SpringerBriefs in Finance

SpringerBriefs present concise summaries of cutting-edge research and practical applications across a wide spectrum of fields. Featuring compact volumes of 50 to 125 pages, the series covers a range of content from professional to academic. Typical topics might include: a timely report of state-of-the art analytical techniques, a bridge between new research results, as published in journal articles, and a contextual literature review, a snapshot of a hot or emerging topic, an in-depth case study or clinical example, and a presentation of core concepts that students must understand in order to make independent contributions. SpringerBriefs in Finance showcase emerging theory, empirical research, and practical application in corporate finance, banking, financial management, behavioral finance, financial markets, social and entrepreneurial finance, microfinance, and related fields, from a global author community. Briefs are characterized by fast, global electronic dissemination, standard publishing contracts, standardized manuscript preparation and formatting guidelines, and expedited production schedules.

Mahnoosh Mirghaemi • Karen Wendt

AI Technology in Wealth Management

Leveraging Technology to Transform
Financial Strategies

 Springer

Mahnoosh Mirghaemi
CEO
Colivar Gestion AG
Zug, Zug, Switzerland

Karen Wendt ⓘ
CEO
Sustainable Finance
Cham, Zug, Switzerland

ISSN 2193-1720   ISSN 2193-1739   (electronic)
SpringerBriefs in Finance
ISBN 978-3-031-72222-6   ISBN 978-3-031-72223-3   (eBook)
https://doi.org/10.1007/978-3-031-72223-3

This Springer imprint is published by the registered company Springer Nature Switzerland AG
The registered company address is: Gewerbestrasse 11, 6330 Cham, Switzerland

If disposing of this product, please recycle the paper.

Remember to look up at the stars and not down at your feet. Try to make sense of what you see and wonder about what makes the universe exist. Be curious. And however difficult life may seem, there is always something you can do and succeed at.

It matters that you don't just give up.
Stephen Hawking

Authors' Preamble

Artificial intelligence (AI) is fundamentally transforming our lives in myriad ways, from enhancing daily tasks to revolutionizing entire industries. It is driving creativity, catalyzing industry changes, and reshaping the financial sector. However, the impacts of AI on financial markets, portfolio management, and asset management have not yet been explicitly described and fully valued. This contribution aims to address this gap.

The role of AI in asset and wealth management is profound, even though its influence is currently more visible in other sectors. This preamble offers an eagle's-eye perspective on how AI is transforming various industries. Subsequently, we will delve into a detailed analysis of its impact on financial markets, portfolio engineering, and asset and wealth management.

From a broad view, it is evident that artificial intelligence has significantly infiltrated and influenced numerous aspects of our lives. This brief will explore these transformations, providing valuable insights into the evolving landscape of AI in wealth management.

Streamlining Routine Tasks

AI-powered virtual assistants, such as Siri, Alexa, and Google Assistant, enhance daily routines by managing calendars, setting reminders, and organizing to-do lists. These tools streamline routine tasks, making our lives smoother and more efficient (Morgan State University).[1]

---

[1] Enhancing Everyday Life: How AI is Revolutionizing Your Daily Experience (Morgan State University).

Personalizing Recommendations

AI is significantly impacting healthcare by providing remote consultations, improving patient care through wearable devices, and aiding disease diagnosis with advanced data analysis capabilities (Morgan State University).

Revolutionizing Healthcare

AI is playing a significant role in healthcare by providing remote consultations, enhancing patient care through wearable devices, and aiding in disease diagnosis with big data analysis capabilities (Morgan State University 2024).

Enhancing Communication

AI improves communication by categorizing emails, offering instant customer support through chatbots, and enabling real-time language translation, thereby bridging language gaps (Morgan State University 2024).

The integration of AI into various aspects of life represents a paradigm shift, offering both opportunities and challenges. While AI has the potential to make our lives more convenient and efficient, it also raises important ethical and regulatory issues that must be addressed to harness its benefits responsibly. AI is fueling creativity and innovation, presenting us with the responsibility to seize its opportunities and manage its risks.

From a detailed perspective, generative AI technologies have the potential to automate complex tasks, provide deeper insights, and enhance efficiency in financial operations. For instance, generative AI can summarize financial documents, convert text into visual data, and generate impact analyses from new regulations, assisting finance professionals in making more informed decisions swiftly (McKinsey & Company, 2024,[2] Deloitte United States, 2024).[3] McKinsey reports that many CFOs are exploring or piloting generative AI to streamline operations and gain strategic advantages. AI is expected to revolutionize roles within finance departments, potentially increasing productivity and cost savings, while necessitating new skills for finance professionals. Tasks traditionally performed by humans, such as financial analysis and reporting, are increasingly automated, enabling finance teams to focus on more strategic activities (IBM - United States, 2024).[4]

---

[2] How generative AI can help finance professionals | McKinsey.

[3] The Impact of Generative AI in Finance | Deloitte US.

[4] How generative AI can help finance and accounting professionals—IBM Blog.

According to SAP Concur, AI will significantly improve personalization in financial processes and enhance overall operational efficiency (Concur, 2024).[5]

According to the International Monetary Fund, authors Ghiath Shabsigh and El Bachir Boukherouaa (IMF 2024) discuss the transformative potential and inherent risks of AI in finance. They note that AI, especially generative AI, enhances efficiency and decision-making processes in financial institutions but also introduces new risks such as embedded bias and cyber threats, which could affect financial stability (IMF, 2023).[6] David Mhlanga from the University of Johannesburg examines the role of AI in promoting digital financial inclusion. He underscores how AI technologies help address information asymmetry, enhance risk management, and provide customer support through chatbots, thereby enabling financial inclusion for underserved populations (D. Mhlange, 2020, MDPI).[7]

All this is valuable groundwork for our book. However, we argue that the potential of AI extends far beyond the benefits identified by others. Our central thesis is that AI can democratize asset and wealth management, making wealth creation more accessible to a broader population. We are confident that you will enjoy exploring these new, untapped possibilities with us.

Mahnoosh Mirghaemi
Karen Wendt

---

[5] Travel Expense Management—SAP Concur.

[6] Generative Artificial Intelligence in Finance in: FinTech Notes Volume 2023 Issue 006 (2023) (imf.org).

[7] Industry 4.0 in Finance: The Impact of Artificial Intelligence (AI) on Digital Financial Inclusion.

Introduction

In an era where technology reshapes every facet of our lives, artificial intelligence (AI) stands at the forefront, particularly in wealth management. This brief embarks on a journey to explore the profound implications of AI on financial inclusion, the democratization of access to wealth management services, and the rise of impact investing.

The landscape of wealth management is rapidly evolving, driven by advancements in AI and technology. AI-driven algorithms are dismantling barriers that have traditionally hindered access to financial services, offering tailored solutions to underserved or overlooked individuals and communities. By harnessing the power of big data and machine learning, AI enables personalized financial advice, investment strategies, and risk management techniques that adapt to diverse needs and circumstances.

The democratization of wealth management goes beyond accessibility; it redefines financial decision-making. AI empowers individuals with greater control and transparency over their investments, fostering a culture of responsible investing where environmental, social, and governance (ESG) criteria play a pivotal role. Impact investing, once a niche pursuit, is now a mainstream trend, driven by AI's ability to analyze complex datasets and identify opportunities that deliver both financial returns and positive social or environmental outcomes.

At the helm of this transformation are Dr. Mahnoosh Mirghaemi and Dr. Karen Wendt, whose pioneering work exemplifies the integration of AI with finance.

Dr. Mahnoosh Mirghaemi, CEO of Colivar Gestion AG in Switzerland, revolutionizes trading algorithms through advanced digital signal processing and quantum physics strategies. With a background in Engineering and Mathematics, her innovative approach is enhanced by a PhD from the UK PhD Center in Financial Computing at University College London, recognized by the *Financial Times*. As a Fund Manager and Chief Economist, she leads Colivar Gestion AG, a FINMA-regulated asset management firm, championing sustainable investment strategies that promote financial independence for women and navigate complex market dynamics to address the wealth gap.

Dr. Karen Wendt, CEO of Eccos Impact GmbH and a Professor of International Finance, blends her expertise in behavioral finance, investment banking, and sustainability. She pioneered ESG in investment banking, creating extra-financial risk management departments at UniCredit and HypoVereinsbank. With a PhD from Vienna Modul University in Business and Socio-Economic Sciences, her career spans roles at Deutsche Bank and UniCredit, where she co-created project finance and innovated extra-financial risk management.

Dr. Mirghaemi's and Dr. Wendt's careers are marked by a fervent advocacy for gender equality and sustainable investment. Driven by a passion to break down financial barriers and promote inclusivity within the investment world, their combined efforts highlight the correlation between finance and climate change, advocating for a new investment mindset to mainstream climate finance.

As we navigate this transformative era, understanding the implications of AI in wealth management is crucial. While the benefits—greater inclusivity, enhanced personalization, and a broader societal impact—are clear, challenges such as data privacy, algorithmic bias, and regulatory frameworks must be addressed to ensure equitable advancements.

This brief provides a comprehensive exploration of these themes, drawing insights from thought leaders and technological innovators at the forefront of this revolution. By understanding the intersection of AI and wealth management, we can navigate the complexities of the digital age while striving for a more inclusive, sustainable, and prosperous future for all.

Welcome to the journey of exploring AI in wealth management—a journey that promises to reshape how we manage wealth, invest in our futures, and contribute to a more equitable world.

Intention of this Research

In an era marked by rapid technological advancement, the financial industry stands on the brink of a profound transformation. This book, "AI Technology in Wealth Management," delves into the revolutionary impact of Artificial Intelligence (AI) on the wealth management landscape. This research provides a comprehensive exploration of how AI is reshaping financial strategies, democratizing access to wealth management, and enhancing client experiences.

The Evolving Landscape of Wealth Management

Wealth management has traditionally been a domain reserved for the affluent, characterized by personalized advisory services and comprehensive financial planning. However, the introduction of AI and advanced data analytics is democratizing this field, making professional wealth management accessible to a broader audience. This book begins with a detailed introduction to wealth management, tracing its historical evolution and highlighting its modern practices.

The Integration of AI in Wealth Management

At the core of this transformation is the integration of AI technologies. From data analytics and predictive modeling to automated investment platforms and personalized financial advice, AI is revolutionizing every aspect of wealth management. The book explores:

- **Data Analytics and Predictive Modeling:** How AI leverages big data to provide deep insights, forecast trends, and inform strategic financial decisions.
- **Automated Investment Platforms:** The rise of robo-advisors and algorithmic trading systems, offering cost-effective, efficient, and personalized investment management solutions.
- **Personalization and Customization:** AI's capability to deliver highly personalized financial plans and investment strategies tailored to individual client needs.

Enhancing Efficiency and Accuracy

One of the most significant advantages of AI in wealth management is its ability to enhance operational efficiency and accuracy. By automating routine tasks, reducing costs, and improving the precision of financial strategies, AI-driven systems ensure that financial decisions are based on accurate and reliable data.

Comparing Traditional and AI-Driven Wealth Management

The research also offers a comparative analysis of traditional wealth management and AI-driven approaches. While traditional practices excel in personalized service and building trust through human interaction, they are often limited by higher costs and scalability issues. In contrast, AI-driven wealth management offers efficiency, scalability, and data-driven personalization but may lack the personal touch and emotional support of human advisors. The book suggests that a hybrid model combining both approaches could offer the best of both worlds.

Future Potential and Ethical Considerations

Looking forward, the book discusses the future potential of AI in wealth management, including advancements in AI technology, enhanced client experiences, and improved regulatory compliance and risk management. It also emphasizes the importance of promoting ethical AI practices to ensure transparency, fairness, and accountability in AI-driven decisions.

Call to Action

This book concludes with a call to action for wealth management firms to embrace AI technology, focus on client-centric solutions, commit to continuous improvement, and promote ethical AI practices. By doing so, firms can deliver superior financial solutions and achieve long-term success in an increasingly competitive landscape

July 24, 2024   Mahnoosh Mirghaemi
                                                                                    Karen Wendt

Contents

Chapter 1
Wealth Management and the Three Percent Conondrum

Wealth Management

Wealth management is the comprehensive management of an individual's or entity's financial assets and investments, aiming to grow wealth over time while mitigating risks. It encompasses a wide range of services and strategies tailored to meet specific financial objectives, such as retirement planning, tax optimization, estate planning, and investment management.

The Terrain of Wealth Management

Wealth management traditionally takes place within the realm of private banking and investment advisory services offered by financial institutions such as banks, brokerage firms, and independent financial advisors and asset managers. These professionals utilize their expertise to tailor strategies that align with clients' financial goals, risk tolerance, and time horizon. Access to wealth management services has historically been limited, primarily due to several factors:

- Many wealth management services have high minimum investment requirements, which exclude individuals with modest savings from accessing personalized financial advice and sophisticated investment strategies.
- Understanding wealth management requires financial literacy and awareness, which may not be universally accessible. Lack of education about financial planning and investment options further contributes to the exclusivity of wealth management.
- Access to wealth management often relies on personal networks and referrals. Those outside affluent circles may not have the connections to access reputable advisors or firms.

© The Author(s), under exclusive license to Springer Nature Switzerland AG 2024   1
M. Mirghaemi, K. Wendt, *AI Technology in Wealth Management*, SpringerBriefs
in Finance, https://doi.org/10.1007/978-3-031-72223-3_1

The 3 Percent Conundrum

Statistics indicate that only a small fraction of the global population—roughly 3 percent—are considered affluent or high-net-worth individuals with sufficient wealth to engage in comprehensive wealth management services. This disparity underscores the challenges of wealth inequality and the concentration of financial resources among a privileged few.

Why Only 3 Percent?

The reasons behind this disparity are multifaceted:

- **Income Inequality**: Those with higher incomes have more surplus capital to invest and grow. Wealth begets wealth through compounding returns and asset appreciation. Those who start with more capital have a greater opportunity to accumulate wealth over time.
- **Educational and Institutional Barriers**: Access to quality education, financial literacy programs, and institutional support can either facilitate or hinder wealth accumulation.
- **Inherited Wealth:** A significant portion of wealth is inherited rather than earned. Individuals born into wealthy families often have access to substantial financial resources and opportunities from birth, perpetuating the cycle of wealth.
- **Investment Opportunities**: Affluent individuals often have access to exclusive investment opportunities that are not available to the general public, such as private equity, hedge funds, and real estate investments requiring large minimum investments.
- **Tax Policies**: Favorable tax policies and loopholes can disproportionately benefit high-net-worth individuals, allowing them to preserve and grow their wealth more effectively than those with lower incomes.
- **Social and Professional Networks**: Wealthy individuals often have access to influential social and professional networks that provide opportunities for lucrative business deals, insider information, and advantageous partnerships.
- **Economic Systems and Policies**: Economic systems and policies in many countries tend to favor capital over labor, meaning those who own assets and capital (like stocks, real estate, and businesses) can see their wealth grow faster than those who rely solely on wages.
- **Geographic Disparities**: Wealth distribution can vary significantly based on geographic location. Individuals in developed countries often have more opportunities and support systems for wealth accumulation compared to those in developing countries.
- **Health and Life Expectancy**: Wealthier individuals typically have better access to healthcare and can afford healthier lifestyles, leading to longer life expectancies and more time to accumulate wealth.

- **Political Influence**: High-net-worth individuals often have more political influence, enabling them to advocate for policies that protect and enhance their wealth.
- **Risk Tolerance**: Affluent individuals may have a higher tolerance for financial risk, allowing them to take advantage of more complex and potentially higher-yield investment opportunities.

Evolving Landscape of Wealth Management

The landscape of wealth management is evolving rapidly. Technological advancements, particularly the rise of fintech and robo-advisors, are democratizing access to basic investment services. These platforms offer automated portfolio management and financial planning tools at lower costs, thereby expanding access beyond traditional wealth thresholds.

Regulatory Efforts and Financial Education

Moreover, regulatory efforts and initiatives promoting financial education are aiming to bridge the gap in financial literacy and inclusion. Governments, nonprofits, and private sector entities are collaborating to develop programs that empower individuals with the knowledge and tools to make informed financial decisions and access wealth management services more equitably.

Future of Wealth Management

While challenges persist, the democratization of wealth management through technological innovation and educational initiatives holds promise for a more inclusive financial landscape. By addressing barriers to access and promoting financial literacy, we can strive towards a future where wealth management services are accessible to a broader segment of society, empowering individuals to achieve their financial goals and build sustainable wealth over time.

Definition

Wealth management is an area in banking and asset management and complex field that encompasses a wide range of financial services aimed at managing and growing an individual's or family's wealth. It involves financial planning, investment management, and estate planning, among other services (Ting, 2017). This chapter will introduce the fundamental concepts of wealth management, its scope, and its purpose, setting the stage for a deeper exploration in subsequent chapters.

Wealth management is defined as a consultative process whereby the advisor gleans information about the client's wants and tailors a bespoke strategy utilizing appropriate financial products and services. The objective is to grow, preserve, and ultimately transfer wealth in a manner that meets the client's goals. Wealth management goes beyond mere investment advice to encompass all parts of a person's financial life.

Scope and Purpose

The scope of wealth management is broad and includes several key areas:

1. **Financial Planning**: Developing a roadmap for the client's financial future, considering income, expenses, investments, and risk management.
2. **Investment Management**: Creating and managing a portfolio of investments tailored to the client's risk tolerance and goals.
3. **Tax Planning and Optimization**: Structuring the client's finances to minimize tax liabilities legally.
4. **Estate Planning:** Ensuring that the client's wealth is distributed according to their wishes after their death, including will preparation and trust management.
5. **Retirement Planning**: Helping clients prepare financially for their retirement years.
6. **Risk Management**: Identifying and mitigating financial risks through insurance and other strategies.

The purpose of wealth management is to provide a holistic approach to managing an individual's financial life. It aims to offer peace of mind by ensuring that all aspects of the client's finances are being handled professionally and that their future financial security is being actively managed (Investopedia, 2024).

Historical Context

Wealth management has evolved significantly over the centuries. Historically, wealth management was the purview of the very rich, with services provided by private banks and exclusive financial advisors. The industrial revolution and the subsequent growth of capital markets in the 19th and 20th centuries expanded access to investment opportunities, but comprehensive wealth management services remained largely inaccessible to the average person.

In the late twentieth century, advances in technology and the rise of the financial planning profession began to democratize access to wealth management services. The internet and digital tools have played a crucial role in making information and services available to a broader audience, setting the stage for the next revolution in wealth management: the integration of Artificial Intelligence (AI) (Fig. 1.1).

20 Years of Wealth Management

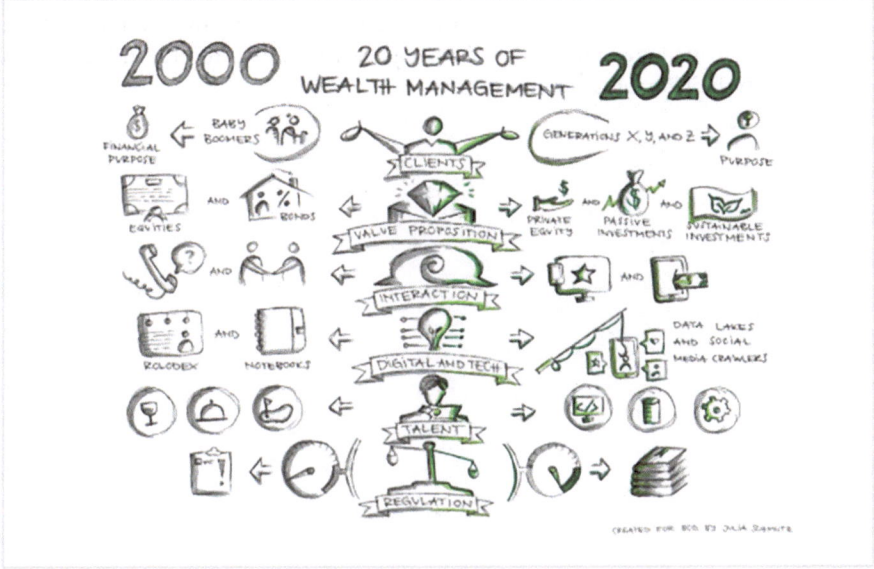

Fig. 1.1 Insights drawn from Boston Consulting Group (BCG) ideation sessions an expert interviews

Modern Practices

Today, wealth management involves a blend of traditional personal advisory services and modern digital tools. Advisors utilize sophisticated software to analyze client data, model financial scenarios, and recommend strategies. There is a growing trend towards personalization, with services tailored to the individual needs and circumstances of each client.

Advisors work closely with clients to develop a deep understanding of their financial goals and preferences, offering bespoke solutions that encompass investments, tax planning, estate planning, and more. This personalized approach is designed to build long-term relationships based on trust and transparency.

The Client Perspective

From the client's viewpoint, wealth management is about achieving financial security and peace of mind. Clients expect their advisors to provide expert guidance, manage their investments prudently, and help them achieve their financial goals. This includes planning for major life events, such as buying a home, funding education, and preparing for retirement.

Clients also value transparency and communication (PwC Consulting Research Paper, 2017). They want to understand how their money is being managed and feel confident that their advisor is acting in their best interest. The integration of digital tools in wealth management has made it easier for clients to stay informed and engaged with their financial planning.

Chapter 2
Wealth Management: A Short Story of Its History and Journey to Modern Times

Wealth management, as a multifaceted discipline, involves more than just managing investments. It encompasses a comprehensive suite of financial services aimed at meeting the diverse needs of clients. In this chapter, we will delve into the historical context and modern practices of wealth management to provide a clear understanding of what this field entails.

Historical Context

The roots of wealth management can be traced back to ancient civilizations, where wealthy individuals sought advice from financial stewards (Brunel, 2015). Over time, as economies evolved and financial markets developed, the role of wealth managers became more defined and specialized.

- **Early Beginnings**: In ancient times, the wealthy relied on trusted advisors to manage their assets, which often included land, livestock, and precious metals. These advisors were responsible for preserving and growing wealth through prudent management and trade.
- **Medieval and Renaissance Periods:** During these periods, the growth of trade and commerce led to the rise of banking families such as the Medici in Italy, who provided a range of financial services, including asset management and investment advice. The concept of managing wealth began to take a more structured form.
- **Industrial Revolution**: The industrial revolution brought about significant economic changes, leading to the accumulation of substantial wealth among industrialists and entrepreneurs. Private banks and financial advisors began offering more sophisticated services to manage and grow this wealth.

© The Author(s), under exclusive license to Springer Nature Switzerland AG 2024
M. Mirghaemi, K. Wendt, *AI Technology in Wealth Management*, SpringerBriefs
in Finance, https://doi.org/10.1007/978-3-031-72223-3_2

- **20th Century:** The advent of modern financial markets, regulatory frameworks, and technological advancements in the 20th century significantly transformed wealth management. The development of mutual funds, the establishment of financial planning as a profession, and the rise of global financial institutions broadened the scope of services available to clients.

Modern Practices

Today, wealth management is a dynamic field that integrates various financial services to provide holistic solutions tailored to individual client needs. Modern wealth management practices are characterized by a client-centric approach, advanced technological tools, and a broad range of financial services.

- **Client-Centric Approach**: Modern wealth management focuses on understanding the unique needs and goals of each client. Advisors work closely with clients to develop personalized strategies that align with their financial objectives, risk tolerance, and time horizons. This involves detailed financial planning, regular reviews, and adjustments to the plan as circumstances change.
- **Comprehensive Services**: Wealth management encompasses a wide array of services, including:
  - **Investment Management:** Crafting and managing diversified portfolios to achieve specific investment goals.
  - **Financial Planning**: Creating detailed plans that address all aspects of a client's financial life, including budgeting, saving, investing, and planning for major life events.
  - **Tax Planning and Optimization**: Structuring finances in a way that minimizes tax liabilities and maximizes after-tax returns.
  - **Estate Planning**: Ensuring the orderly transfer of wealth according to the client's wishes, including the use of wills, trusts, and other legal instruments.
  - **Retirement Planning**: Preparing clients financially for retirement, ensuring they have sufficient income to maintain their desired lifestyle.
  - **Risk Management:** Identifying potential financial risks and implementing strategies to mitigate them, such as insurance and diversification.
- **Technological Integration**: The integration of technology in wealth management has revolutionized the way services are delivered. Financial advisors now use sophisticated software to analyze data, model financial scenarios, and provide real-time insights. This technology enhances the accuracy and efficiency of wealth management services.
- **Regulatory Compliance**: Wealth managers operate within a complex regulatory environment designed to protect clients and ensure the integrity of financial markets. Compliance with regulations such as the Dodd-Frank Act, the Fiduciary Rule, and various international standards is essential for maintaining trust and credibility.

Key Components of Wealth Management

Wealth management involves several key components that work together to provide a comprehensive service:

- **Financial Planning**: This is the foundation of wealth management. It involves understanding the client's financial situation, setting goals, and creating a plan to achieve those goals. Financial planning covers areas such as budgeting, saving, investing, and risk management.
- **Investment Management:** This involves creating and managing an investment portfolio tailored to the client's goals and risk tolerance. It includes asset allocation, portfolio diversification, and ongoing monitoring and rebalancing.
- **Tax Planning:** Effective tax planning strategies can significantly impact the client's overall financial health. Wealth managers work to minimize tax liabilities and maximize after-tax returns through careful planning and optimization.
- **Estate Planning:** Estate planning ensures that the client's wealth is transferred according to their wishes upon death. It involves the use of legal instruments such as wills, trusts, and powers of attorney to manage and distribute assets.
- **Retirement Planning**: Preparing for retirement is a critical aspect of wealth management. Advisors help clients accumulate sufficient savings and create income strategies to support their desired lifestyle in retirement.
- **Risk Management**: Identifying and managing risks is essential to protecting wealth. This includes assessing insurance needs, diversifying investments, and implementing strategies to mitigate potential financial risks.

Client Engagement and Relationship Management

Building and maintaining strong client relationships is a cornerstone of successful wealth management. This involves regular communication, transparency, and a deep understanding of the client's needs and preferences.

- **Regular Communication**: Wealth managers maintain regular contact with clients through meetings, phone calls, and digital channels. This ensures that clients are informed about their financial situation and any changes to their plan.
- **Transparency**: Clients value transparency in the management of their wealth. Advisors provide clear and detailed reports on the performance of investments, fees, and any changes to the financial plan.
- **Personalized Service:** Wealth management is highly personalized. Advisors take the time to understand the client's goals, preferences, and circumstances, tailoring their services to meet these specific needs.

The Role of Technology

Technology plays a crucial role in modern wealth management. From data analytics to robo-advisors, technological advancements have made wealth management more efficient, accurate, and accessible.

- **Data Analytics**: Advanced data analytics tools help wealth managers analyze market trends, assess risk, and make informed investment decisions. These tools provide deeper insights into the client's financial situation and the broader economic environment.
- **Robo-Advisors:** Robo-advisors are automated platforms that provide investment management services with minimal human intervention. They use algorithms to create and manage portfolios based on the client's risk tolerance and goals. This technology has made wealth management more accessible to a broader audience (Singh & Kaur, 2017).
- **Digital Platforms**: Digital platforms allow clients to access their financial information, view reports, and communicate with their advisor from anywhere. These platforms enhance the client experience by providing real-time access to information and services.

Limitations of Robo-Advisors

While Robo-advisors offer several benefits, they also have notable limitations (Singh & Kaur, 2017):

- **Lack of Personal Guidance**: Robo-advisors operate based on programmed algorithms and cannot provide the personal, tailored advice that human advisors can. They are limited by their programming and cannot adapt to unique or complex situations that fall outside of their algorithms. They also cannot offer the friendly, reassuring advice that many investors seek during volatile market conditions.
- **Limited Scope**: Investors often require advice that goes beyond investment management, encompassing areas such as financial planning, tax strategies, and estate planning. These comprehensive needs are typically best addressed by seasoned human advisors who can integrate various aspects of a client's financial life.
- **Absence of Human Interaction:** Many investors value face-to-face meetings with their advisors. This personal interaction is not possible with robo-advisors, which can be a significant drawback for those who prefer or require direct, personal communication.
- **Adaptability to Changes**: When investment rules or policies change, robo-advisors need to be reprogrammed to incorporate these changes. This process can take time, money, and effort, whereas human advisors can often adapt to such changes more quickly and start using the new information immediately.

In conclusion, wealth management is a comprehensive field that combines financial planning, investment management, tax optimization, estate planning, retirement planning, and risk management. Modern wealth management practices focus on providing personalized, client-centric services supported by advanced technology. However, it is essential to recognize the limitations of robo-advisors and the critical role that human advisors continue to play in offering nuanced, personalized, and comprehensive financial advice.

Chapter 3
The Place of Wealth Management in the Modern Financial Landscape

Wealth management holds a crucial place in today's financial landscape, providing individuals and families with the tools and strategies necessary to navigate complex financial markets, achieve financial goals, and secure their financial futures. This chapter will explore the economic impact of wealth management, its importance from the client's perspective, and the role it plays in the broader financial ecosystem.

Economic Impact

- **Facilitating Capital Markets:**
  Wealth management plays a significant role in the functioning of capital markets. By pooling the resources of individual investors and channeling them into various investment vehicles, wealth managers contribute to the liquidity and efficiency of financial markets. This, in turn, supports economic growth and stability by enabling businesses to raise capital for expansion and innovation.
- **Promoting Economic Stability:**
  Wealth management helps promote economic stability by encouraging prudent financial behavior and long-term planning. By advising clients on diversified investment strategies and risk management, wealth managers help mitigate the impact of economic downturns on individual investors. This stability at the individual level can contribute to broader economic resilience.
- **Supporting Innovation and Entrepreneurship:**
  Through investment in startups and emerging technologies, wealth managers play a crucial role in supporting innovation and entrepreneurship. By allocating capital to promising ventures, wealth managers help drive technological advancements and economic progress.

© The Author(s), under exclusive license to Springer Nature Switzerland AG 2024
M. Mirghaemi, K. Wendt, *AI Technology in Wealth Management*, SpringerBriefs in Finance, https://doi.org/10.1007/978-3-031-72223-3_3

Client Perspective

- **Financial Security and Peace of Mind:**
  One of the primary benefits of wealth management from the client's perspective is financial security. By providing expert guidance on investments, savings, and risk management, wealth managers help clients build and preserve wealth. This financial security provides peace of mind, knowing that their financial future is being professionally managed.
- **Achieving Financial Goals:**
  Wealth management helps clients articulate and achieve their financial goals, whether it's buying a home, funding education, retiring comfortably, or leaving a legacy. Advisors work with clients to develop tailored financial plans that align with their objectives and time horizons, ensuring that they stay on track to meet their goals.
- **Personalized Financial Advice:**
  Clients value the personalized advice provided by wealth managers. Unlike generic financial advice, wealth management involves a deep understanding of the client's unique circumstances, preferences, and goals. This personalized approach ensures that the financial strategies implemented are well-suited to the client's specific needs.
- **Simplifying Financial Complexity:**
  The financial world can be complex and overwhelming. Wealth managers simplify this complexity by providing clear, actionable advice and managing the various aspects of the client's financial life. This allows clients to focus on their personal and professional lives without being burdened by financial worries.

Role in the Broader Financial Ecosystem

- **Financial Intermediaries:**
  Wealth managers act as financial intermediaries, connecting individual investors with investment opportunities. By leveraging their expertise and market knowledge, wealth managers help clients make informed investment decisions and access a wide range of financial products.
- **Enhancing Financial Literacy:**
  Wealth management also plays a role in enhancing financial literacy. Through education and regular communication, wealth managers help clients understand complex financial concepts and make better financial decisions. This increased financial literacy can have positive ripple effects throughout the economy.
- **Encouraging Responsible Investing:**
  In recent years, there has been a growing emphasis on responsible investing and Environmental, Social, and Governance (ESG) criteria. Wealth managers are at the forefront of this movement, advising clients on how to incorporate ESG fac-

tors into their investment strategies. This not only aligns investments with the client's values but also promotes sustainable business practices.

- **Adapting to Regulatory Changes:**
  The wealth management industry is highly regulated, with a focus on protecting investors and ensuring market integrity. Wealth managers must stay abreast of regulatory changes and adapt their practices accordingly. This compliance ensures that clients are protected and that the industry operates in a transparent and ethical manner.

In Conclusion, Wealth management is integral to the modern financial landscape, providing essential services that benefit individuals, families, and the broader economy. From facilitating capital markets and promoting economic stability to providing personalized financial advice and enhancing financial literacy, wealth management plays a vital role in ensuring financial security and prosperity.

As we move forward, the importance of wealth management will continue to grow, driven by technological advancements, changing client needs, and a dynamic regulatory environment. The next chapter will explore the traditional practices of wealth management, setting the stage for understanding how AI is revolutionizing this field.

Chapter 4
How Does a Traditional Wealth Management Process and Its Practices Work?

Wealth management, as a profession, has undergone significant changes over the years. Despite the advancements in technology and the emergence of AI-driven solutions, traditional wealth management practices still form the foundation of the industry. This chapter will delve into these traditional practices, including manual processes and their inherent limitations.

Manual Processes

Traditional wealth management relies heavily on manual processes that are labor-intensive and require significant expertise and time. These processes are centered around personalized client interaction and bespoke financial advice.

Figure 4.1 offers a visual representation of the advisory services provided by wealth management, highlighting the contemporary focus on robo-advisory. It illustrates that the current perspective on robo-advisory is almost exclusively centered on the advisory process itself, rather than on traditional advisory activities. This shift underscores the innovative approach of robo-advisors, which leverage technology to streamline and enhance the advisory process, setting them apart from conventional methods (Cocca, 2016).

1. **Client Onboarding and Profiling:**

   - **Initial Consultation**: The wealth management process begins with an in-depth initial consultation where the advisor gathers comprehensive information about the client's financial situation, goals, risk tolerance, and personal preferences. This often involves filling out detailed questionnaires and holding multiple meetings.

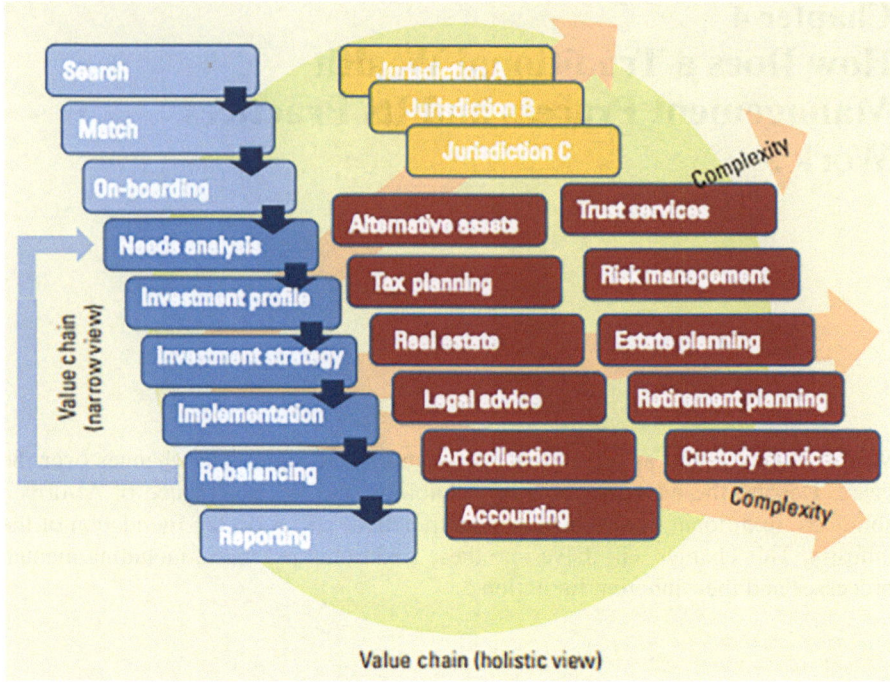

Fig. 4.1 Visual representation of the advisory services provided by wealth management. (Source: Cocca, 2016)

- **Risk Assessment:** Advisors conduct thorough risk assessments to understand the client's risk tolerance. This involves evaluating the client's financial stability, investment knowledge, and emotional response to market volatility.

2. **Financial Planning:**

- **Goal Setting:** Advisors work with clients to set clear, achievable financial goals. This includes short-term objectives, such as saving for a home or a child's education, and long-term goals, such as retirement planning and estate planning.
- **Strategy Development**: Based on the client's goals and risk profile, the advisor develops a comprehensive financial strategy. This strategy includes investment planning, tax optimization, retirement planning, and estate planning.

3. **Investment Management:**

- **Portfolio Construction:** Advisors construct a diversified investment portfolio tailored to the client's risk tolerance and financial goals. This involves selecting a mix of asset classes, such as equities, bonds, real estate, and alternative investments.

- **Active Management:** Traditional wealth management often involves active portfolio management, where advisors make regular buy and sell decisions based on market conditions, economic trends, and the client's evolving needs.

4. **Performance Monitoring and Reporting:**

- **Regular Reviews:** Advisors conduct regular reviews of the client's financial plan and investment portfolio to ensure alignment with their goals. These reviews typically occur quarterly or annually.
- **Performance Reports:** Clients receive detailed performance reports that provide insights into the performance of their investments, including returns, asset allocation, and any changes made to the portfolio.

Limitations of Traditional Practices

While traditional wealth management practices offer personalized and bespoke services, they come with several limitations that can impact efficiency and effectiveness.

1. **Time-Consuming Processes:**

- **Manual Data Collection:** The process of gathering and analyzing client information manually is time-consuming and prone to errors. Advisors spend a significant amount of time collecting data, filling out forms, and updating records.
- **Strategy Implementation:** Implementing financial strategies and making investment decisions manually requires considerable time and effort. This can delay the execution of investment opportunities and adjustments.

2. **High Costs:**

- **Advisory Fees:** Traditional wealth management services are often expensive, with high advisory fees and commissions. These costs can be a barrier for individuals with smaller portfolios, limiting access to professional financial advice.
- **Operational Costs:** The reliance on manual processes increases operational costs for wealth management firms. These costs are often passed on to clients, making traditional services less affordable.

3. **Limited Scalability:**

- **Advisor Capacity:** Traditional wealth management is heavily dependent on the advisor's capacity to manage a finite number of clients. This limits the scalability of the business, as advisors can only handle a certain number of clients effectively.
- **Customization Challenges:** While personalization is a key strength of traditional wealth management, it also poses a challenge in terms of scalability.

Customizing financial plans and investment strategies for each client individually can be resource-intensive.

4. **Subjectivity and Bias:**

- **Advisor Judgment:** Traditional wealth management relies heavily on the advisor's judgment and expertise. While this can be beneficial, it also introduces subjectivity and potential biases in decision-making.
- **Emotional Factors:** Advisors and clients may be influenced by emotional factors, such as fear and greed, which can impact investment decisions. This can lead to suboptimal outcomes, particularly during periods of market volatility.

The Human Touch

Despite the limitations, traditional wealth management practices offer significant benefits, particularly in terms of the human touch and personalized service.

1. **Personal Relationships:**

- **Trust and Confidence:** Building personal relationships with clients fosters trust and confidence. Clients often value the reassurance and emotional support provided by their advisor, especially during challenging financial times.
- **Deep Understanding:** Advisors who know their clients well can provide more tailored and relevant advice. This deep understanding of the client's needs and preferences enhances the overall effectiveness of the financial plan.

2. **Bespoke Solutions:**

- **Tailored Strategies:** Traditional wealth management excels in providing bespoke financial solutions that are closely aligned with the client's unique circumstances and goals.
- **Holistic Approach:** Advisors take a holistic view of the client's financial situation, integrating various aspects of financial planning, investment management, tax optimization, and estate planning.

In Conclusion, Traditional wealth management practices have formed the bedrock of the industry for decades, offering personalized and bespoke services that cater to the unique needs of each client. However, these practices are not without their limitations, including time-consuming processes, high costs, limited scalability, and potential biases.

As we move forward, the integration of advanced technologies, particularly AI, promises to address many of these limitations while retaining the benefits of personalized service. The next chapter will explore the emergence of AI in wealth management, setting the stage for understanding how this technology is revolutionizing the field.

Chapter 5
Embracing the Future: Emergence of AI in Wealth Management

The financial industry is undergoing a profound transformation with the advent of artificial intelligence (AI). This chapter explores the emergence of AI in wealth management, examining the technological advancements that have driven this change, the current market trends, and the potential implications for the industry.

Technological Advancements

1. **Artificial Intelligence and Machine Learning:**

   - **Definition and Scope:** AI refers to the simulation of human intelligence in machines programmed to think and learn like humans. Machine learning, a subset of AI, involves the use of algorithms and statistical models to enable computers to improve their performance on a specific task through data and experience.
   - **Applications in Finance:** AI and machine learning are being applied in various aspects of finance, including fraud detection, credit scoring, algorithmic trading, and, more recently, wealth management.

2. **Big Data:**

   - **Data Explosion:** The exponential growth of data, driven by digitalization, social media, and IoT (Internet of Things), has provided a wealth of information that can be harnessed for financial decision-making.
   - **Data Analytics:** Advanced data analytics tools enable wealth managers to analyze vast amounts of data quickly and accurately, uncovering patterns and insights that were previously unattainable.

M. Mirghaemi, K. Wendt, *AI Technology in Wealth Management*, SpringerBriefs in Finance, https://doi.org/10.1007/978-3-031-72223-3_5

3. **Deep Learning:**

   - **Neural Networks:** Deep learning, a subset of machine learning, involves neural networks with many layers that can learn from vast amounts of unstructured data. This technology is particularly useful in recognizing patterns, such as market trends and client behavior.
   - **Financial Forecasting:** Deep learning algorithms can analyze historical data to make accurate financial forecasts, assisting in portfolio management and risk assessment.

4. **Natural Language Processing (NLP):**

   - **Understanding Text and Speech:** NLP enables computers to understand, interpret, and generate human language. In wealth management, NLP is used to analyze news articles, financial reports, and social media to gauge market sentiment and make informed investment decisions.
   - **Chatbots and Virtual Assistants:** NLP powers chatbots and virtual assistants that provide clients with real-time information and personalized financial advice.

Market Trends

1. **Rise of Robo-Advisors:**

   - **Automated Investment Platforms:** Robo-advisors are AI-driven platforms that provide automated, algorithm-based portfolio management services with minimal human intervention. They use clients' financial information, risk tolerance, and investment goals to create and manage portfolios.
   - **Accessibility and Affordability:** Robo-advisors have made wealth management services more accessible and affordable, particularly for individuals with smaller portfolios. They offer lower fees compared to traditional advisory services.

2. **Personalization and Customization:**

   - **Tailored Financial Advice:** AI enables wealth managers to provide highly personalized financial advice by analyzing individual client data and preferences. This level of customization enhances the client experience and improves investment outcomes.
   - **Client Engagement:** AI-driven tools help advisors engage with clients more effectively, offering insights and recommendations that are relevant to their specific financial situation.

3. **Enhanced Risk Management:**

   - **Predictive Analytics:** AI uses predictive analytics to assess and manage risks more effectively. By analyzing historical data and market trends, AI can identify potential risks and suggest strategies to mitigate them.

- **Real-Time Monitoring:** AI systems provide real-time monitoring of investment portfolios, allowing for quick adjustments in response to market changes.

4. **Integration with Traditional Services:**

- **Hybrid Models:** Many wealth management firms are adopting a hybrid model that combines AI-driven tools with traditional advisory services. This approach leverages the efficiency and accuracy of AI while maintaining the personalized touch of human advisors.
- **Augmenting Human Advisors:** AI acts as an augmentation tool for human advisors, providing them with deeper insights and analytics to enhance their decision-making process.

Implications for the Industry

1. **Operational Efficiency:**

- **Automation:** AI automates routine tasks, such as data entry, portfolio rebalancing, and performance reporting, freeing up advisors to focus on more complex and strategic activities.
- **Cost Reduction:** The automation of processes reduces operational costs, enabling wealth management firms to offer services at lower fees.

2. **Enhanced Client Experience:**

- **24/7 Service:** AI-driven tools provide clients with 24/7 access to financial information and advice, improving convenience and responsiveness.
- **Interactive Platforms:** Interactive platforms, powered by AI, engage clients through personalized content, real-time updates, and educational resources.

3. **Data-Driven Decision Making:**

- **Insight Generation:** AI analyzes vast amounts of data to generate actionable insights, helping advisors make informed decisions and provide more accurate financial advice.
- **Improved Accuracy:** The precision of AI-driven analytics reduces the likelihood of human error, enhancing the overall accuracy of financial planning and investment strategies.

4. **Regulatory Compliance:**

- **Compliance Monitoring:** AI systems can monitor transactions and activities for compliance with regulatory requirements, reducing the risk of non-compliance and associated penalties.
- **Reporting and Documentation:** Automated reporting and documentation tools ensure that all regulatory requirements are met efficiently and accurately.

In conclusion, the emergence of AI in wealth management marks a significant shift in how financial services are delivered. Technological advancements in AI, big data, deep learning, and NLP are transforming the industry, making wealth management more efficient, personalized, and accessible. Market trends, such as the rise of robo-advisors and the integration of AI with traditional services, highlight the potential for AI to enhance both operational efficiency and client experience.

As we continue to explore the transformative impact of AI in wealth management, the next chapter will delve into specific ways AI is revolutionizing the industry, including data analytics and predictive modeling, automated investment platforms, and the personalization and customization of financial advice.

Chapter 6
How AI Is Transforming Wealth Management

Artificial intelligence (AI) is revolutionizing wealth management by introducing new capabilities and efficiencies that were previously unimaginable. This chapter will explore the various ways AI is transforming the industry, focusing on data analytics and predictive modeling, automated investment platforms, and the personalization and customization of financial advice.

Data Analytics and Predictive Modeling

1. **Harnessing Big Data:**
   - **Data Collection**: AI systems can gather and process vast amounts of data from diverse sources, including financial markets, economic indicators, social media, and client behaviors. This data provides a comprehensive view of market conditions and client preferences.
   - **Data Integration**: AI integrates data from multiple sources to create a unified and coherent dataset. This holistic view enables wealth managers to make more informed decisions.

2. **Predictive Analytics:**
   - **Market Predictions**: AI algorithms analyze historical market data to identify patterns and trends. These predictive models can forecast market movements, helping wealth managers anticipate changes and adjust strategies accordingly.
   - **Client Behavior:** By analyzing client data, AI can predict future behaviors and preferences. This allows wealth managers to proactively address client needs and enhance satisfaction.

© The Author(s), under exclusive license to Springer Nature Switzerland AG 2024
M. Mirghaemi, K. Wendt, *AI Technology in Wealth Management*, SpringerBriefs
in Finance, https://doi.org/10.1007/978-3-031-72223-3_6

3. **Risk Assessment:**

- **Risk Modeling:** AI uses complex algorithms to assess the risk associated with different investment strategies. These models consider a wide range of factors, including market volatility, economic indicators, and individual client risk tolerance.
- **Real-Time Monitoring:** AI systems continuously monitor market conditions and portfolio performance, providing real-time risk assessments. This enables wealth managers to respond swiftly to potential risks.

Automated Investment Platforms

1. **Robo-Advisors:**

- **Automated Portfolio Management:** Robo-advisors use AI algorithms to manage investment portfolios automatically. They create and maintain a diversified portfolio based on the client's risk tolerance, financial goals, and investment horizon.
- **Cost Efficiency:** By automating portfolio management, robo-advisors offer services at a lower cost compared to traditional advisors. This makes wealth management more accessible to a broader audience.

2. **Algorithmic Trading:**

- **High-Frequency Trading:** AI-driven algorithmic trading systems can execute trades at high speeds, taking advantage of short-term market opportunities. These systems use complex algorithms to analyze market data and make split-second trading decisions. The trading process (Fig. 6.1) can be split into three major areas (Nuti et al., 2011).:

  - **Pre-trade analysis** involves using algorithms to evaluate financial data or news to determine the properties of an asset. This can range from simple company valuation methods to advanced AI techniques that forecast asset price volatility by scanning news. The output is used by human traders to make trading decisions, but it does not generate trade signals on its own.
  - **Trading signal generation** automates the creation of trade signals, often used by systematic asset managers and trading institutions. While the signal is generated automatically, execution is typically manual due to the need for discretionary input or market liquidity issues. This level of automation is generally applied to most trading activities except high-frequency trading, which requires complete automation.
  - **Trade execution** can either optimize human-made trading decisions or fully automate trade placements on exchanges. In agency trading, the algorithm optimizes execution, whereas in proprietary trading, the entire process may be automated. The degree of automation in trade execution often defines the classification of algorithmic trading systems.

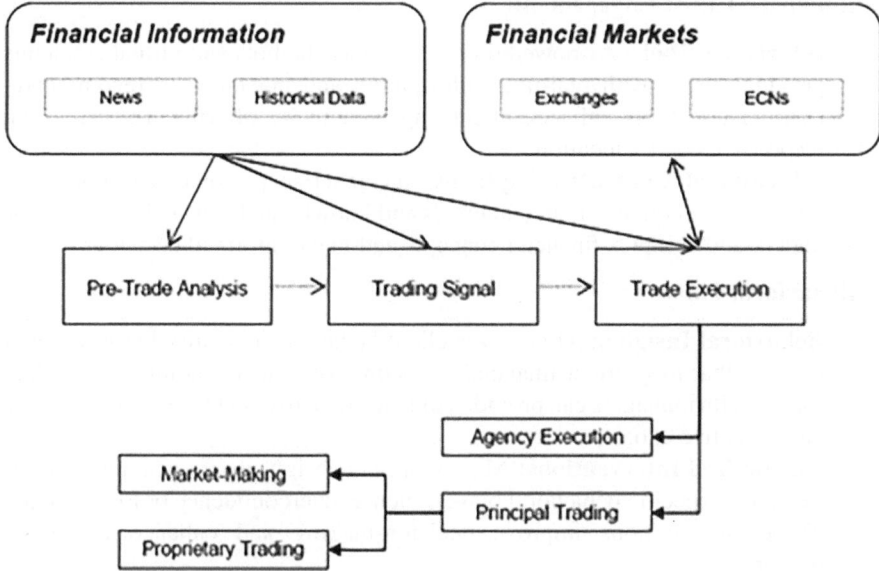

Fig. 6.1 Taxonomy of algorithmic trading systems

- **Reduced Human Error:** Automated trading reduces the potential for human error and emotional decision-making, leading to more consistent and objective trading strategies.

3. **Rebalancing and Optimization:**

   - **Automated Rebalancing:** AI systems automatically rebalance portfolios to maintain the desired asset allocation. This ensures that the portfolio remains aligned with the client's risk tolerance and investment goals.
   - **Portfolio Optimization:** AI algorithms analyze portfolio performance and make adjustments to optimize returns. This involves reallocating assets, selecting new investments, and minimizing costs.

Personalization and Customization

1. **Tailored Financial Advice:**

   - **Client Profiling:** AI creates detailed profiles of clients based on their financial data, preferences, and behaviors. This enables wealth managers to provide highly personalized advice that is tailored to each client's unique needs.
   - **Dynamic Adjustments:** AI systems continuously update client profiles with new data, allowing for dynamic adjustments to financial plans and investment strategies.

2. **Enhanced Client Engagement:**

- **Interactive Tools:** AI-powered tools, such as chatbots and virtual assistants, provide clients with real-time information and personalized recommendations. These tools enhance client engagement by offering interactive and responsive communication.
- **Educational Content:** AI systems can generate personalized educational content based on the client's interests and knowledge level. This helps clients understand complex financial concepts and make informed decisions.

3. **Behavioral Finance:**

- **Behavioral Insights:** AI analyzes client behavior to identify biases and tendencies that may affect financial decisions. By understanding these behaviors, wealth managers can provide guidance to help clients make more rational and objective choices.
- **Customized Interventions:** AI systems can design customized interventions to address specific behavioral biases, such as overconfidence or loss aversion. These interventions improve decision-making and enhance investment outcomes.

Enhancing Efficiency and Accuracy

1. **Streamlining Operations:**

- **Process Automation:** AI automates routine tasks, such as data entry, transaction processing, and report generation. This streamlines operations and reduces the administrative burden on wealth managers.
- **Cost Reduction:** Automation leads to significant cost savings by reducing the need for manual labor and minimizing errors. These savings can be passed on to clients in the form of lower fees.

2. **Improving Accuracy:**

- **Data Precision:** AI systems analyze large datasets with high precision, reducing the likelihood of errors. This improves the accuracy of financial forecasts and investment strategies.
- **Consistent Decision-Making:** AI-driven decision-making is consistent and objective, free from human biases and emotional influences. This leads to more reliable and effective financial strategies.

3. **Regulatory Compliance:**

- **Compliance Monitoring:** AI systems monitor transactions and activities to ensure compliance with regulatory requirements. This reduces the risk of non-compliance and associated penalties.

- **Automated Reporting:** AI automates the generation of compliance reports, ensuring that all regulatory requirements are met accurately and efficiently.

In conclusion, AI is transforming wealth management by introducing advanced data analytics, predictive modeling, automated investment platforms, and personalized financial advice. These technologies enhance operational efficiency, improve accuracy, and provide clients with a more personalized and engaging experience. As AI continues to evolve, its impact on wealth management will only grow, offering new opportunities for innovation and improvement.

In the next chapter, we will delve deeper into the specific aspects of data analytics and predictive modeling, exploring how these technologies are used to drive better investment decisions and enhance risk management.

Chapter 7
Data Analytics and Predictive Modeling Transform Asset and Wealth Management

Data analytics and predictive modeling represent a significant leap forward in wealth management, offering capabilities far beyond those of traditional methods. By leveraging vast amounts of data quickly and efficiently, these technologies enable more informed decision-making and accurate forecasting. At the core of the AI revolution in wealth management, data analytics and predictive modeling provide deep insights, forecast trends, and inform strategic financial decisions. This chapter delves into their utilization, focusing on their roles, methodologies, and impact on investment strategies and risk management.

Predictive analysis today heavily relies on AI and machine learning algorithms, which process and interpret vast datasets at unprecedented speeds and accuracies unattainable through manual analysis. The fundamental advantage of data analytics and predictive modeling over traditional wealth management lies in their ability to harness data-driven insights, personalize client experiences, and manage risks more effectively. These capabilities, significantly enhanced by AI and machine learning technologies, have revolutionized the field by making predictive analysis faster, more accurate, and scalable.

Without AI, the depth and speed of predictive analysis seen today would be unachievable. This marks a fundamental shift in how wealth management is practiced and perceived in the modern era. Let us explore the underlying reasons for this transformation.

Role of Big Data in Wealth Management

Big data analysis can merge various data sources and come up with a prediction where these sources and different analytical methods are combined and pondered. From data sources to integration and analysis, a streamlined prediction space opens up for decision making. The datasets help humans to make informed decisions and

M. Mirghaemi, K. Wendt, *AI Technology in Wealth Management*, SpringerBriefs in Finance, https://doi.org/10.1007/978-3-031-72223-3_7

not be driven by emotional or behavioural bias. The models can include the prediction of client behavior and are able to detect both behavioral and market anomalies.

1. **Data Sources:**

   - **Market Data:** Includes stock prices, trading volumes, interest rates, and other financial indicators. This data is essential for understanding market dynamics and making investment decisions.
   - **Economic Data:** Encompasses macroeconomic indicators such as GDP, unemployment rates, inflation, and consumer confidence. These metrics help in assessing economic conditions and potential market impacts.
   - **Client Data:** Comprises demographic information, financial statements, transaction histories, and behavioral data. This data provides insights into client preferences and risk tolerance.

2. **Data Integration:**

   - **Combining Multiple Sources:** AI systems integrate data from various sources to create a comprehensive dataset. This holistic view enables more accurate analysis and better decision-making.
   - **Data Cleaning:** Before analysis, data must be cleaned and standardized to ensure accuracy. This involves removing duplicates, correcting errors, and ensuring consistency across different datasets.

Predictive Analytics

Predictive analysis entails market forecasting, client behavior prediction and uses as variety of analytical methods, methodologies and tools.

1. **Market Forecasting:**

   - **Historical Data Analysis:** AI analyzes historical market data to identify patterns and trends. By understanding past behaviors, predictive models can forecast future market movements.
   - **Algorithmic Predictions:** Machine learning algorithms, such as neural networks and regression models, are used to predict stock prices, market trends, and economic indicators.

2. **Client Behavior Prediction:**

   - **Behavioral Analysis:** AI examines client behavior patterns, such as spending habits and investment choices, to predict future actions. This helps in tailoring financial advice and product offerings.
   - **Risk Profiling:** Predictive models assess a client's risk tolerance based on their financial history and behavioral data. This allows for the creation of personalized investment strategies that align with the client's risk profile.

In the following let us have a look into the methodologies used.

Methodologies in Data Analytics

1. **Descriptive Analytics:**

   - **Data Summarization:** Descriptive analytics involves summarizing historical data to understand what has happened in the past. This provides a baseline for further analysis and decision-making.
   - **Visualization Tools:** Charts, graphs, and dashboards are used to present data in a clear and understandable format. These tools help wealth managers and clients visualize financial performance and trends.

2. **Diagnostic Analytics:**

   - **Identifying Causes:** Diagnostic analytics goes a step further by identifying the causes of past events. This involves examining correlations and relationships within the data to understand why something happened.
   - **Anomaly Detection:** AI can detect anomalies in financial data, such as unusual trading volumes or unexpected market movements. Identifying these anomalies helps in mitigating potential risks.

3. **Predictive Analytics:**

   - **Forecasting Models:** Predictive analytics uses statistical models and machine learning algorithms to forecast future events. These models are trained on historical data and continuously updated with new information.
   - **Scenario Analysis:** AI generates different financial scenarios based on various assumptions and inputs. This helps wealth managers assess potential outcomes and plan accordingly.

4. **Prescriptive Analytics:**

   - **Actionable Recommendations:** Prescriptive analytics provides actionable recommendations based on predictive insights. It suggests specific actions to achieve desired outcomes, such as adjusting asset allocations or rebalancing portfolios.
   - **Optimization Models:** These models help in optimizing investment strategies by considering multiple objectives and constraints. AI can recommend the best course of action to maximize returns and minimize risks.

Impact of Analytics Methodologies on Investment Strategies

The application of descriptive, diagnostic, predictive, and prescriptive analytics profoundly influences investment strategies, offering unique insights and capabilities that enhance wealth management practices:

Descriptive Analytics: Data Summarization

Descriptive analytics involves summarizing historical data to help wealth managers understand past performance and trends. This foundational knowledge is crucial for setting benchmarks and evaluating investment strategies based on historical outcomes.

- **Visualization Tools:** Charts, graphs, and dashboards visually represent financial data, making it easier for wealth managers and clients to identify patterns and trends. This clarity facilitates informed decision-making by highlighting key areas of interest or concern in investment portfolios.

Diagnostic Analytics: Identifying Causes and Anomaly Detection

Diagnostic analytics goes beyond summarizing data to identify the causes of past successes or failures in investments. By analyzing correlations and relationships within historical data, wealth managers can adjust strategies to capitalize on successful patterns or mitigate risks associated with unsuccessful ones.

- **Anomaly Detection:** AI-powered diagnostic analytics can detect anomalies in financial data, such as unexpected market movements or irregular trading patterns. Identifying these anomalies early allows wealth managers to take proactive measures to protect investments.

Predictive Analytics: Forecasting Models and Scenario Analysis

Predictive analytics uses statistical models and machine learning algorithms to forecast future market trends, asset prices, and economic conditions. These forecasts provide valuable insights into potential investment opportunities and risks, guiding wealth managers in making strategic decisions.

- **Scenario Analysis:** AI-driven scenario analysis generates multiple future scenarios based on different assumptions and inputs. Wealth managers can simulate the impact of various economic or market conditions on investment portfolios, helping them prepare robust strategies that are resilient to different scenarios.

Prescriptive Analytics: Actionable Recommendations and Optimization

Prescriptive analytics takes predictive insights a step further by recommending specific actions to achieve desired outcomes. For example, it may suggest adjusting asset allocations, rebalancing portfolios, or diversifying investments based on forecasted market conditions.

- **Optimization Models:** AI-driven optimization models consider multiple objectives and constraints to recommend the most optimal investment strategies. These models help wealth managers maximize returns while managing risks effectively, taking into account factors such as risk tolerance, liquidity needs, and investment goals.

Overall Impact: Enhanced Decision-Making and Personalization

The integration of these analytics methodologies leads to better and faster decisions, early risk detection, and personalized investment strategies. Together, these capabilities empower wealth managers to make informed, data-driven decisions.

- **Comprehensive View:** These analytics provide a comprehensive view of past performance, identify root causes of outcomes, forecast future scenarios, and recommend precise actions to achieve financial objectives.
- **Risk Mitigation:** By detecting anomalies and forecasting potential risks, analytics help mitigate financial risks associated with investments. This proactive approach improves portfolio resilience and safeguards against unexpected market fluctuations.
- **Personalization:** Analytics enable personalized investment strategies tailored to individual client goals, risk tolerance levels, and financial circumstances. This customization enhances client satisfaction and improves investment outcomes.

In essence, the integration of descriptive, diagnostic, predictive, and prescriptive analytics in wealth management enhances the precision, effectiveness, and responsiveness of investment strategies, ultimately striving towards optimizing returns and managing risks in a dynamic and complex financial landscape.

Let us now decompose the impact from a portfolio manager's perspective and highlight the benefits of AI usage.

Enhanced Decision-Making

- **Data-Driven Insights:** AI provides wealth managers with data-driven insights that enhance decision-making. These insights are based on rigorous analysis and objective data, reducing the influence of emotions and biases.
- **Real-Time Analysis:** AI systems offer real-time analysis of market conditions and portfolio performance. This enables wealth managers to make timely and informed decisions.

Portfolio Management

- **Asset Allocation:** AI assists in determining the optimal asset allocation based on the client's risk tolerance and investment goals. This involves diversifying investments across different asset classes to minimize risk and maximize returns.
- **Dynamic Rebalancing:** Predictive models continuously monitor the portfolio and recommend rebalancing actions to maintain the desired asset allocation. This ensures that the portfolio remains aligned with the client's objectives.

Risk Management

- **Risk Assessment:** AI evaluates the risk associated with different investment strategies by analyzing historical data and market conditions. This helps in identifying potential risks and implementing mitigation strategies.
- **Stress Testing:** Predictive models simulate various market scenarios to assess the impact on the portfolio. This helps wealth managers understand how the portfolio might perform under different conditions and make necessary adjustments.

Challenges and Considerations

In the realm of wealth management and financial analytics, several critical challenges revolve around data quality, cleanliness, privacy concerns, and model reliability. These challenges can significantly impact the effectiveness and trustworthiness of analytics-driven decision-making processes:

1. **Data Quality:**
   - **Accuracy and Completeness:** The accuracy and completeness of data are critical for effective analytics. Inaccurate or incomplete data can lead to erroneous conclusions and suboptimal decisions.

- **Data Privacy:** Ensuring the privacy and security of client data is paramount. Wealth managers must comply with data protection regulations and implement robust security measures to safeguard sensitive information.

2. **Model Reliability:**

- **Algorithm Bias:** AI models can sometimes exhibit biases based on the data they are trained on. It's important to regularly review and update models to ensure they provide unbiased and accurate predictions.
- **Transparency:** The complexity of AI algorithms can make them difficult to understand and explain. Wealth managers need to ensure transparency in their use of AI and be able to explain the rationale behind AI-driven decisions to clients.

3. **Integration with Human Expertise:**

- **Augmenting, Not Replacing:** AI should be seen as a tool to augment human expertise, not replace it. Wealth managers should use AI-driven insights to enhance their decision-making and provide better service to clients.
- **Continuous Learning:** Both AI systems and human advisors must continuously learn and adapt to changing market conditions and client needs. This requires ongoing training and development for advisors and regular updates for AI models.

In conclusion, data analytics and predictive modeling are transforming wealth management by providing deep insights, enhancing decision-making, and optimizing investment strategies. These technologies leverage the power of big data to forecast trends, assess risks, and deliver personalized financial advice. While there are challenges to address, the integration of AI with human expertise promises to revolutionize the industry, making wealth management more efficient, accurate, and client-centric.

The next chapter will delve into automated investment platforms, exploring how AI-driven technologies such as robo-advisors and algorithmic trading are changing the landscape of wealth management.

Chapter 8
Automated Investment Platforms and Their Benefits

Automated investment platforms, powered by advanced AI technologies, have revolutionized the asset management landscape. These platforms offer cost-effective, efficient, and personalized investment management solutions, making wealth management accessible to a broader audience. This chapter explores the various types of automated investment platforms, their functionalities, and their impact on the industry.

Key Benefits of Automated Data Platforms in Asset Management

Automated data platforms provide numerous advantages that significantly enhance asset management operations. These benefits include increased efficiency, accuracy, scalability, and cost-effectiveness, which collectively transform the way wealth managers handle data and make investment decisions.

Efficiency and Time Savings

Automated data platforms drastically reduce the time and effort required for data collection, integration, processing, and analysis. Tasks that traditionally took hours or days can now be completed in minutes or even seconds with automated workflows. This efficiency allows wealth managers and analysts to focus more on strategic decision-making rather than mundane data processing tasks.

M. Mirghaemi, K. Wendt, *AI Technology in Wealth Management*, SpringerBriefs in Finance, https://doi.org/10.1007/978-3-031-72223-3_8

Enhanced Data Accuracy and Consistency

These platforms maintain high levels of data accuracy and consistency by minimizing human errors associated with manual data entry and processing. By standardizing data formats and validation rules, automated platforms ensure that data quality meets predefined standards, enhancing the reliability of analytical insights and reports.

Scalability and Performance

Automated platforms are designed to scale, capable of handling large volumes of data from diverse sources without compromising performance. As the volume and complexity of data grow, these platforms can effortlessly scale up to accommodate increasing data processing needs, supporting the evolving requirements of wealth management firms.

Real-Time Data Analytics and Reporting

By automating data capture and processing, these platforms enable real-time data analytics and reporting. Wealth managers can access up-to-date information on market trends, portfolio performance, and client preferences, empowering timely and informed decision-making. This agility is crucial in dynamic financial markets where quick responses to changing conditions can make a significant difference.

Seamless Integration

Automated data platforms facilitate seamless integration with various data sources, systems, and applications used in wealth management. They support data connectivity across internal departments, external partners, and client interfaces, fostering collaboration and improving operational efficiency across the organization.

Data Governance and Regulatory Compliance

These platforms help enforce data governance policies and regulatory compliance requirements effectively. They enable auditing capabilities, data lineage tracking, and automated alerts for anomalies or deviations from compliance standards, thereby reducing risks associated with data breaches, errors, and regulatory penalties.

Cost Savings and Operational Efficiency

While the initial setup and integration costs may be significant, automated data platforms can deliver long-term cost savings by optimizing resource allocation, reducing operational overheads, and minimizing the need for manual interventions. They contribute to overall cost efficiency through improved productivity and enhanced operational effectiveness.

Summary

In summary, the primary benefit of automated data platforms in asset management and investing lies in their ability to transform data into actionable insights swiftly, accurately, and at scale. By automating repetitive tasks, ensuring data accuracy, enabling real-time insights, and enhancing compliance capabilities, these platforms empower wealth managers to make informed decisions, deliver superior client experiences, and remain competitive in a rapidly evolving financial landscape.

Automated investment platforms have not only democratized access to professional financial services but also set new standards for efficiency, accuracy, and responsiveness in wealth management. As the industry continues to evolve, these platforms will play an increasingly vital role in shaping the future of asset management.

Main Applications of Automated Platforms

Robo-advisory, algorithmic trading (algo trading), and hybrid models are distinct approaches used in the realm of wealth and asset management, do-it yourself investors and financial markets participants, each with its unique characteristics and objectives. Here are the differences between these three models:

Robo-Advisors

1. **Introduction to Robo-Advisors:**
   - **Definition:** Robo-advisors are online platforms that provide automated, algorithm-driven financial planning services with little to no human supervision. They create and manage investment portfolios based on clients' financial goals and risk tolerance.
   - **History:** The first robo-advisors emerged in the wake of the 2008 financial crisis, offering a low-cost alternative to traditional financial advisors. Companies like Betterment and Wealthfront were pioneers in this space.

2. **Functionality:**

   - **Client Onboarding:** Clients begin by completing an online questionnaire that assesses their financial situation, goals, risk tolerance, and investment preferences. Based on this information, the robo-advisor recommends a suitable investment strategy.
   - **Portfolio Construction:** The platform constructs a diversified portfolio using exchange-traded funds (ETFs) and other low-cost investment products. Asset allocation is determined by the client's risk profile and investment horizon.
   - **Automated Rebalancing:** Robo-advisors automatically rebalance portfolios to maintain the desired asset allocation. This involves buying and selling assets to keep the portfolio aligned with the client's risk tolerance and investment goals.
   - **Tax-Loss Harvesting:** Some robo-advisors offer tax-loss harvesting, a strategy to minimize taxes by selling losing investments to offset capital gains from winning investments.

3. **Advantages:**

   - **Cost-Effective:** Robo-advisors typically charge lower fees compared to traditional advisors, making investment management more affordable.
   - **Accessibility:** These platforms democratize access to professional investment management, allowing individuals with smaller portfolios to benefit from sophisticated financial strategies.
   - **Convenience:** Clients can manage their investments online, with easy access to their portfolios and real-time updates.

4. **Challenges:**

   - **Limited Personal Interaction:** The lack of human advisors can be a drawback for clients who prefer personalized guidance and face-to-face interactions.
   - **Algorithm Dependence:** Robo-advisors rely on algorithms that may not account for every nuance of an individual's financial situation. There is also a risk of over-reliance on historical data, which may not always predict future market conditions accurately.

Algorithmic Trading

1. **Introduction to Algorithmic Trading:**

   - **Definition:** Algorithmic trading uses computer algorithms to execute trades at high speeds and volumes. These algorithms are programmed to follow specific instructions for placing trades to generate profits at a speed and frequency that is impossible for a human trader.

- **History:** Algorithmic trading has been around since the 1970s, but it gained significant traction in the 2000s with advances in technology and data processing capabilities.

2. **Functionality:**

   - **Pre-Trade Analysis:** Algorithms analyze large volumes of market data to identify trading opportunities. This includes price trends, trading volumes, and historical patterns.
   - **Execution:** Once a trading opportunity is identified, the algorithm executes trades automatically. This can involve buying or selling large quantities of assets in a fraction of a second.
   - **Post-Trade Analysis**: After executing trades, algorithms evaluate the outcomes and refine their strategies for future trades.

3. **Advantages:**

   - **Speed and Efficiency:** Algorithmic trading can execute trades at lightning speed, taking advantage of fleeting market opportunities.
   - **Reduced Human Error:** Automated systems reduce the risk of human error and emotional decision-making, leading to more consistent trading performance.
   - **Cost Reduction:** By automating the trading process, firms can reduce operational costs and improve profit margins.

4. **Challenges:**

   - **Market Impact:** High-frequency trading can lead to market volatility and has been associated with events like the "flash crash" of 2010.
   - **Technical Failures:** Algorithmic trading systems are susceptible to technical failures and software glitches, which can result in significant financial losses.
   - **Regulatory Scrutiny:** The use of automated trading systems is subject to regulatory oversight to ensure fair and transparent market practices.

Hybrid Models

1. **Introduction to Hybrid Models:**

   - **Definition:** Hybrid models combine the benefits of robo-advisors and human financial advisors. They offer automated investment management along with access to human advisors for personalized guidance and support.
   - **Emergence:** Many traditional wealth management firms have adopted hybrid models to stay competitive and meet the evolving needs of clients.

2. **Functionality:**

- **Automated and Human Interaction:** Clients benefit from automated port-folio management and rebalancing, while also having the option to consult with human advisors for more complex financial planning needs.
- **Personalized Advice:** Human advisors provide personalized advice on retire-ment planning, estate planning, tax strategies, and other areas that require a nuanced understanding of the client's financial situation.
- **Client Engagement:** Hybrid models offer a high level of client engagement through a combination of digital tools and personal interactions.

3. **Advantages:**

- **Best of Both Worlds:** Clients get the efficiency and cost-effectiveness of automated platforms along with the personalized service and expertise of human advisors.
- **Flexibility:** Hybrid models cater to a wide range of clients, from those who prefer digital interactions to those who value personal relationships with their advisors.
- **Enhanced Client Trust:** The involvement of human advisors helps build trust and confidence, especially for clients with complex financial needs.

4. **Challenges:**

- **Cost Management:** Maintaining both automated systems and human advi-sors can be costly for wealth management firms. Balancing these costs while offering competitive fees is a challenge.
- **Integration:** Ensuring seamless integration between automated platforms and human advisors requires robust technology and coordination.

Impact on the Wealth Management Industry

The introduction and adoption of robo-advisory platforms, algorithmic trading (algo trading), and hybrid models have significantly impacted the financial markets and wealth management industries. These technologies have influenced various aspects, including accessibility, efficiency, risk management, and client relationships.

Algorithmic trading enhances market efficiency by facilitating faster trade exe-cution and reducing price discrepancies. This narrows bid-ask spreads and improves liquidity in financial markets. Robo-advisors, on the other hand, promote efficient asset allocation and portfolio diversification among retail investors, contributing to a more balanced and rationalized investment landscape.

Algo trading strategies also contribute to increased trading volumes, particularly in liquid markets, as algorithms can execute trades swiftly based on predefined cri-teria. This liquidity provision benefits market participants by reducing transaction costs and improving market depth.

Automated platforms, including robo-advisors, offer greater transparency in investment decisions and portfolio management. Clients can access real-time information about their investments and understand the rationale behind automated recommendations. However, they have the potential to exacerbate short-term market volatility, especially during periods of high-frequency trading or algorithmic reactions to news events. Conversely, automated risk management features in algo trading can mitigate volatility by automatically adjusting positions in response to market conditions.

Robo-advisors democratize access to asset management services by offering low-cost, automated investment solutions. This makes financial advice and portfolio management accessible to a broader segment of retail investors who may not meet traditional high-net-worth thresholds.

Hybrid models combine the efficiency of robo-advisory with the personalized touch of human advisors, catering to clients who seek a balance between automated efficiency and human expertise. They provide a personalized client experience by integrating automated portfolio management with human advisory services. This dual approach allows for customized financial planning based on individual client goals, risk tolerance, and preferences. Enhanced client engagement is facilitated through interactive digital platforms that provide real-time insights, educational resources, and personalized recommendations.

In conclusion, robo-advisory platforms, algorithmic trading, and hybrid models have reshaped the financial markets and wealth management industries by enhancing efficiency, accessibility, and client engagement. While these technologies offer numerous benefits such as cost savings, market liquidity, and personalized advice, they also present challenges related to market volatility, regulatory compliance, and the need for ongoing technological innovation. As these automated platforms continue to evolve, their impact on financial markets and wealth management practices will continue to shape the future of investment management globally.

These are the most significant impacts that will increase only over time:

1. **Market Accessibility:**

   - **Broader Reach:** Automated investment platforms have expanded the reach of wealth management services, making them accessible to a wider audience, including millennials and individuals with smaller investment portfolios.
   - **Financial Inclusion:** These platforms promote financial inclusion by lowering the barriers to entry for professional investment management.

2. **Industry Disruption:**

   - **Competitive Landscape:** The rise of robo-advisors and algorithmic trading has disrupted the traditional wealth management industry, forcing firms to innovate and adopt new technologies to stay competitive.
   - **Fee Compression:** Increased competition from low-cost automated platforms has led to fee compression, putting pressure on traditional firms to reduce their fees and offer more value-added services.

3. **Client Expectations:**

   - **Demand for Transparency:** Clients expect greater transparency in how their investments are managed. Automated platforms provide real-time updates and detailed reports, meeting this demand.
   - **Preference for Digital Solutions**: The digital-first approach of automated platforms aligns with the preferences of tech-savvy clients who value convenience and accessibility.

4. **Regulatory Considerations:**

   - **Compliance Requirements:** Automated investment platforms must comply with regulatory requirements to ensure client protection and market integrity. This includes adhering to fiduciary standards and providing clear disclosures.
   - **Risk Management:** Regulators are increasingly focused on the risk management practices of automated trading systems to prevent market disruptions and protect investors.
     The adoption of automated platforms necessitates adherence to regulatory guidelines and data privacy laws, especially concerning client information security, algorithmic transparency, and fair market practices.
     Regulatory frameworks continue to evolve to address the implications of automated trading and digital advisory services, ensuring consumer protection and market integrity.

In conclusion, automated investment platforms, including robo-advisors and algorithmic trading systems, have significantly transformed the wealth management industry. These platforms offer cost-effective, efficient, and personalized investment solutions, making wealth management services more accessible to a broader audience. Hybrid models that combine automated systems with human advisors provide the best of both worlds, enhancing client engagement and trust.

As the industry continues to evolve, the integration of advanced AI technologies will further enhance the capabilities of automated investment platforms, driving innovation and improving client outcomes. The next chapter will explore the personalization and customization of financial advice, highlighting how AI enables wealth managers to deliver tailored solutions that meet the unique needs of each client.

Chapter 9
The Triple Win Factor: Enhancing Efficiency and Accuracy

The integration of AI in wealth management has significantly enhanced operational efficiency and accuracy. This chapter explores how AI-driven technologies streamline processes, reduce costs, and improve the precision of financial strategies and decisions.

Process Optimization and Automated Functionalities

Automated functionalities such as rebalancing, trade execution, and reporting provide a "triple win" scenario, benefiting clients, portfolio managers, and regulators by enhancing efficiency, transparency, and compliance in wealth management and financial markets.

Client Benefits

1. **Cost Reduction:** Automated processes reduce operational costs for wealth management firms, enabling them to pass on savings to clients through lower fees and expenses.
2. **Error Minimization:** Automation minimizes human errors in trade execution and rebalancing, reducing potential losses and optimizing investment returns.
3. **Enhanced Performance:** Automated rebalancing ensures portfolios are regularly adjusted to maintain target asset allocations, helping clients stay aligned with their investment goals and risk tolerance, thus optimizing portfolio performance over time.

© The Author(s), under exclusive license to Springer Nature Switzerland AG 2024   47
M. Mirghaemi, K. Wendt, *AI Technology in Wealth Management*, SpringerBriefs
in Finance, https://doi.org/10.1007/978-3-031-72223-3_9

4. **Timely Trade Execution:** Automated trade execution allows for swift and precise implementation of investment decisions based on market conditions, ensuring clients capitalize on favorable opportunities without delays.
5. **Real-Time Data:** Automated reporting provides clients with immediate access to comprehensive and accurate performance metrics, portfolio insights, and transaction details. This transparency enhances trust and empowers clients to make informed decisions about their investments.
6. **Personalized Experience:** Automated platforms can customize investment strategies and reporting formats to meet individual client preferences and financial objectives, offering a personalized wealth management experience.

Portfolio Manager Benefits

1. **Time Savings:** Automated processes free portfolio managers from routine tasks, allowing them to focus on strategic decision-making, client relationships, and portfolio analysis.
2. **Scalability:** Portfolio managers can efficiently handle larger volumes of client accounts and transactions, supporting business growth without a proportional increase in operational resources.
3. **Automated Compliance:** Automated systems ensure regulatory compliance by aligning trades and portfolio decisions with established guidelines and risk management protocols, reducing regulatory risks and potential penalties.
4. **Risk Management:** Automated risk monitoring and reporting tools help portfolio managers identify and mitigate risks promptly, safeguarding client assets and enhancing overall portfolio resilience.
5. **Service Quality:** Leveraging automated rebalancing, trade execution, and reporting capabilities allows portfolio managers to deliver superior service quality, responsiveness, and transparency to clients, fostering long-term relationships and client loyalty.

Regulatory Benefits

1. **Market Integrity:** Automated trade execution ensures fairness and transparency in financial markets by reducing the potential for market manipulation or insider trading.
2. **Regulatory Compliance:** Automated reporting facilitates timely and accurate regulatory filings, disclosures, and audit trails, promoting adherence to regulatory standards and enhancing market integrity.
3. **Enhanced Oversight:** Automated systems provide regulators with real-time access to standardized and reliable data, supporting effective market oversight, surveillance, and enforcement activities.

4. **Cybersecurity:** Automated platforms incorporate robust cybersecurity measures to protect sensitive client information and financial data, mitigating risks associated with cyber threats and data breaches.

Process optimization and automated functionalities in asset and wealth management create a "triple win" scenario by enhancing efficiency, transparency, and compliance across the financial ecosystem. Clients benefit from cost savings, enhanced performance, and greater control over their investments. Portfolio managers gain operational efficiency, improved risk management capabilities, and enhanced client satisfaction. Regulators benefit from improved market integrity, regulatory compliance, and enhanced data transparency. Together, these benefits contribute to a more resilient, transparent, and efficient wealth management industry that effectively serves the interests of all stakeholders.

Let us have a deeper look into how this functions:

Streamlining Operations

1. **Process Automation:**

    - **Routine Tasks:** AI automates routine tasks such as data entry, transaction processing, and report generation. This reduces the administrative burden on wealth managers, allowing them to focus on more strategic activities.
    - **Client Onboarding:** AI streamlines the client onboarding process by automating the collection and analysis of client information. This ensures a faster and more efficient onboarding experience.

2. **Portfolio Management:**

    - **Automated Rebalancing:** AI systems automatically rebalance portfolios to maintain the desired asset allocation. This involves buying and selling assets to keep the portfolio aligned with the client's risk tolerance and investment goals.
    - **Trade Execution:** AI-driven platforms execute trades automatically, based on pre-defined algorithms and market conditions. This ensures timely and efficient trade execution, minimizing the impact of market fluctuations.

3. **Compliance and Reporting:**

    - **Regulatory Compliance:** AI monitors transactions and activities to ensure compliance with regulatory requirements. This includes tracking and reporting on transactions, managing documentation, and maintaining audit trails.
    - **Automated Reporting:** AI generates compliance reports automatically, ensuring that all regulatory requirements are met accurately and efficiently. This reduces the risk of non-compliance and associated penalties.

Cost Reduction

1. **Operational Costs:**

   - **Reduced Labor Costs:** By automating routine tasks, AI reduces the need for manual labor, leading to significant cost savings. Wealth management firms can operate more efficiently with smaller teams (Bührer, 2005).
   - **Efficiency Gains**: Automation leads to efficiency gains by streamlining processes and reducing the time required to complete tasks. This allows firms to serve more clients without proportionally increasing costs.

2. **Investment Costs:**

   - **Lower Fees:** AI-driven platforms, such as robo-advisors, typically charge lower fees compared to traditional advisors. This makes investment management more affordable for clients and expands access to professional financial services.
   - **Cost-Effective Solutions:** AI enables wealth managers to offer cost-effective solutions, such as passive investment strategies and ETF-based portfolios, which have lower management fees.

Improving Accuracy

1. **Data Precision:**

   - **Advanced Analytics:** AI systems analyze large datasets with high precision, identifying patterns and trends that may not be apparent to human analysts. This improves the accuracy of financial forecasts and investment strategies.
   - **Error Reduction:** Automated processes reduce the likelihood of human error in data entry, analysis, and reporting. This ensures that financial decisions are based on accurate and reliable data.

2. **Consistent Decision-Making:**

   - **Algorithmic Strategies:** AI-driven algorithms make decisions based on pre-defined rules and data analysis. This ensures consistent and objective decision-making, free from human biases and emotional influences.
   - **Continuous Improvement:** AI systems continuously learn and adapt based on new data and feedback. This iterative process leads to ongoing improvements in the accuracy and effectiveness of financial strategies.

Enhancing Financial Planning

1. **Personalized Financial Plans:**

   - **Tailored Advice:** AI analyzes individual client data to create personalized financial plans that align with their goals, risk tolerance, and preferences. This ensures that financial advice is relevant and actionable.
   - **Dynamic Adjustments:** AI continuously updates financial plans based on changes in the client's financial situation and market conditions. This allows for timely adjustments to strategies and ensures that plans remain aligned with the client's objectives.

2. **Goal Tracking:**

   - **Progress Monitoring:** AI tools help clients track their progress towards financial goals, providing real-time updates and insights. This helps clients stay on track and make informed decisions.
   - **Automated Alerts:** AI systems can send automated alerts and notifications when clients are off-track or when adjustments to their financial plans are needed. This proactive approach enhances client engagement and satisfaction.

Enhanced Risk Management

1. **Risk Assessment:**

   - **Predictive Analytics:** AI uses predictive analytics to assess the risk associated with different investment strategies. This involves analyzing historical data, market trends, and economic indicators to identify potential risks.
   - **Stress Testing:** AI models simulate various market scenarios to assess the impact on the portfolio. This helps wealth managers understand how the portfolio might perform under different conditions and make necessary adjustments.

2. **Real-Time Monitoring:**

   - **Market Surveillance:** AI continuously monitors market conditions and portfolio performance, providing real-time risk assessments. This enables wealth managers to respond swiftly to potential risks and take preventive measures.
   - **Anomaly Detection:** AI systems can detect anomalies in financial data, such as unusual trading volumes or unexpected market movements. Identifying these anomalies helps in mitigating potential risks and protecting client assets.

Case Studies and Examples

1. **Case Study: Operational Efficiency in Robo-Advisors:**
   - **Wealthfront:** Wealthfront uses AI to automate various aspects of portfolio management, including asset allocation, rebalancing, and tax-loss harvesting. This automation reduces operational costs and enhances accuracy.
   - **Betterment:** Betterment's robo-advisor platform leverages AI to provide cost-effective and efficient investment management. The platform's automation capabilities allow it to offer lower fees and personalized advice to a broad client base.

2. **Example: AI in Compliance and Reporting:**
   - **BlackRock Aladdin:** BlackRock's Aladdin platform uses AI to manage risk, monitor compliance, and generate automated reports. This comprehensive system enhances operational efficiency and ensures regulatory compliance.
   - **Goldman Sachs Marquee:** Goldman Sachs' Marquee platform employs AI to provide clients with real-time analytics and automated reporting. This improves the accuracy and efficiency of financial planning and investment management.

In conclusion, AI-driven technologies have significantly enhanced efficiency and accuracy in asset and wealth management. By streamlining operations, reducing costs, and improving the precision of financial strategies, AI enables wealth managers to deliver better outcomes for their clients. The automation of routine tasks, real-time monitoring, and advanced analytics ensure that financial decisions are based on accurate and reliable data.

As the wealth management industry continues to evolve, the integration of AI will further enhance operational efficiency and accuracy, driving innovation and improving client satisfaction. The next chapter will explore the key differences between traditional and AI-driven wealth management, highlighting the advantages and challenges of each approach.

Chapter 10
Key Differences Between Traditional and AI Wealth Management and Why Customers Should Care

The wealth management industry is experiencing a paradigm shift with the integration of AI technologies. While traditional wealth management practices have long been the cornerstone of financial advising, AI-driven approaches are redefining the landscape. This chapter explores the key differences between traditional and AI wealth management, highlighting their respective advantages and challenges. Let us first look into the paradigm shifts.

Human Interaction vs. Automation

1. **Human Interaction in Traditional Wealth Management:**

   - **Personal Relationships:** Traditional wealth management relies heavily on personal relationships between advisors and clients. Advisors spend considerable time understanding clients' needs, goals, and preferences, offering bespoke advice based on their professional judgment.
   - **Trust and Rapport:** The human touch fosters trust and rapport, which are crucial for client retention and satisfaction. Clients often value the reassurance and emotional support provided by their advisors, especially during market volatility.

2. **Automation in AI Wealth Management:**

   - **Algorithm-Driven Decisions:** AI-driven wealth management utilizes algorithms to analyze data and make investment decisions. These systems can process vast amounts of information quickly and accurately, offering data-driven insights and recommendations.
   - **Efficiency and Scalability:** Automation enhances efficiency and scalability, allowing wealth managers to serve more clients with fewer resources. AI

M. Mirghaemi, K. Wendt, *AI Technology in Wealth Management*, SpringerBriefs in Finance, https://doi.org/10.1007/978-3-031-72223-3_10

systems can perform tasks such as portfolio rebalancing, tax optimization, and risk assessment without human intervention.

Personalized Service vs. Personalization Through AI

1. **Personalized Service in Traditional Wealth Management:**

   - **Custom Advice:** Traditional advisors provide personalized advice based on a deep understanding of the client's financial situation and life circumstances. This includes tailored investment strategies, tax planning, estate planning, and more.
   - **Holistic Approach:** Advisors take a holistic view of the client's finances, integrating various aspects of financial planning to create comprehensive solutions.

2. **Personalization through AI:**

   - **Data-Driven Personalization:** AI-driven systems use data analytics to create highly personalized financial plans and investment strategies. These systems continuously update client profiles with new data, ensuring that advice remains relevant and tailored to the client's current needs.
   - **Behavioral Insights:** AI can analyze client behavior to identify biases and preferences, providing personalized interventions to improve decision-making. This level of personalization is data-driven and can adapt in real-time to changes in the client's financial situation.

Decision-Making Processes

1. **Advisor Expertise in Traditional Wealth Management:**

   - **Professional Judgment:** Traditional advisors rely on their expertise and experience to make investment decisions. They consider a wide range of factors, including market conditions, economic indicators, and individual client circumstances.
   - **Qualitative Analysis:** Advisors use qualitative analysis to assess the potential impact of non-quantifiable factors, such as geopolitical events or changes in government policy, on investment strategies.

2. **AI-Driven Decision-Making:**

   - **Quantitative Analysis:** AI systems primarily use quantitative analysis to make investment decisions. They analyze large datasets to identify patterns, trends, and correlations that inform their strategies.

- **Predictive Modeling:** AI uses predictive modeling to forecast market movements and assess risk. These models are based on historical data and continuously learn from new information to improve accuracy.

Client Engagement and Communication

1. **Traditional Client Engagement:**

   - **Regular Meetings:** Traditional advisors engage with clients through regular meetings, phone calls, and emails. These interactions help build strong relationships and ensure that clients are informed about their financial situation.
   - **Customized Reports:** Advisors provide customized reports that detail portfolio performance, investment strategies, and financial planning updates.

2. **AI-Enhanced Client Engagement:**

   - **Interactive Platforms:** AI-driven platforms offer interactive tools such as chatbots and virtual assistants that provide real-time information and personalized recommendations. Clients can access their financial information anytime, anywhere.
   - **Automated Alerts and Notifications:** AI systems send automated alerts and notifications based on market conditions and client-specific triggers. This proactive communication keeps clients informed and engaged.

Cost Structures

1. **Cost Structures in Traditional Wealth Management:**

   - **High Fees:** Traditional wealth management services often come with high fees, including advisory fees, management fees, and commissions. These costs can be a barrier for individuals with smaller portfolios.
   - **Operational Costs:** The reliance on human advisors and manual processes increases operational costs, which are typically passed on to clients.

2. **Cost Structures in AI Wealth Management:**

   - **Lower Fees:** AI-driven platforms, such as robo-advisors, offer lower fees compared to traditional services. The automation of processes reduces operational costs, allowing for more affordable services.
   - **Efficiency Gains:** AI enhances operational efficiency by automating routine tasks and reducing the need for manual labor. This leads to cost savings that benefit clients.

Adaptability and Flexibility

1. **Traditional Wealth Management:**

   - **Personal Adaptability:** Traditional advisors can adapt their strategies based on personal interactions and a deep understanding of the client's evolving needs. This flexibility is rooted in the advisor's ability to interpret qualitative information.
   - **Response Time:** While adaptable, the response time in traditional wealth management can be slower due to the manual nature of analysis and decision-making.

2. **AI Wealth Management:**

   - **Real-Time Adaptability:** AI systems can adapt in real-time to changes in market conditions and client data. This ensures that investment strategies are continuously optimized based on the latest information.
   - **Scalability and Consistency:** AI provides consistent service quality and can easily scale to accommodate more clients without compromising on personalization or efficiency.

Challenges and Considerations

1. **Challenges in Traditional Wealth Management:**

   - **Human Error and Bias:** Traditional wealth management is susceptible to human error and biases, which can impact decision-making and investment outcomes.
   - **Limited Scalability:** The reliance on human advisors limits the scalability of traditional wealth management services. Advisors can only manage a finite number of clients effectively.

2. **Challenges in AI Wealth Management:**

   - **Algorithm Dependence:** AI-driven systems depend on the quality of their algorithms and data. Poorly designed algorithms or inaccurate data can lead to suboptimal decisions.
   - **Lack of Personal Touch:** The absence of human interaction in AI-driven wealth management can be a drawback for clients who value personal relationships and bespoke advice.

In conclusion, traditional and AI-driven wealth management approaches each have their unique advantages and challenges. Traditional wealth management excels in personalized service, building trust through human interaction, and providing holistic financial advice. However, it is limited by higher costs, human biases, and scalability issues.

AI-driven wealth management offers efficiency, scalability, and data-driven personalization (Kaal, 2021), making it more accessible and affordable. While it enhances accuracy and operational efficiency, it may lack the personal touch and emotional support provided by human advisors.

As the wealth management industry continues to evolve, a hybrid approach that combines the strengths of both traditional and AI-driven methods may emerge as the optimal solution. This approach can leverage AI's efficiency and scalability while maintaining the personalized service and trust that clients value.

The next chapter will conclude our exploration of AI in wealth management, summarizing key insights and discussing the future potential of AI-driven financial strategies.

Customers should care about these paradigm shifts because they directly influence how their financial resources are managed, the level of service they receive, and the alignment of their investments with personal values and long-term goals. Staying informed about these shifts allows customers to make educated decisions, leverage emerging opportunities, and navigate potential risks in an evolving financial landscape effectively.

Chapter 11
Conclusion: Harnessing the Power of AI in Wealth Management

The integration of artificial intelligence (AI) in wealth management marks a significant transformation in the financial industry. AI's ability to analyze vast amounts of data, automate processes, and provide personalized financial advice offers numerous advantages over traditional wealth management practices (Devan et al., 2023). This chapter summarizes the key insights from our exploration of AI in wealth management and discusses the future potential of AI-driven financial strategies.

Summary of Key Insights

1. **Emergence and Impact of AI:**

   - AI has revolutionized wealth management by introducing efficiency, accuracy, and scalability. Technologies such as data analytics, predictive modeling, and automated investment platforms have transformed how financial services are delivered and consumed.

2. **Data Analytics and Predictive Modeling:**

   - AI leverages big data to provide deep insights and make accurate financial forecasts. Predictive modeling helps wealth managers anticipate market movements and client behaviors, enabling proactive and informed decision-making.

3. **Automated Investment Platforms:**

   - Platforms like robo-advisors and algorithmic trading systems offer cost-effective and efficient investment management solutions. These platforms democratize access to professional financial services, making them available to a broader audience.

M. Mirghaemi, K. Wendt, *AI Technology in Wealth Management*, SpringerBriefs in Finance, https://doi.org/10.1007/978-3-031-72223-3_11

4. **Personalization and Customization:**

   - AI enables a high degree of personalization by analyzing individual client data to create tailored financial plans and investment strategies. This enhances client satisfaction and engagement by delivering relevant and action-able advice.

5. **Enhancing Efficiency and Accuracy:**

   - Automation of routine tasks, real-time monitoring, and advanced analytics improve operational efficiency and reduce costs. AI-driven systems ensure that financial decisions are based on accurate and reliable data, minimizing human error and biases.

6. **Comparison with Traditional Wealth Management:**

   - While traditional wealth management excels in providing personalized ser-vice through human interaction, it is limited by higher costs and scalability issues. AI-driven approaches offer efficiency, scalability, and data-driven per-sonalization but may lack the personal touch and emotional support of human advisors.

Future Potential of AI in Wealth Management

1. **Advancements in AI Technology:**

   - Continuous advancements in AI technology will further enhance its capabili-ties in wealth management. Improved algorithms, increased computational power, and access to larger datasets will drive more accurate predictions and more effective financial strategies.

2. **Integration of AI and Human Expertise:**

   - The future of wealth management lies in the integration of AI and human expertise. Hybrid models that combine AI-driven tools with the personalized service of human advisors will offer the best of both worlds, providing clients with efficient and tailored financial solutions.

3. **Enhanced Client Experience:**

   - AI will continue to enhance the client experience by offering interactive and engaging platforms. Clients will benefit from real-time insights, personalized content, and proactive communication, leading to greater satisfaction and loyalty.

4. **Regulatory Compliance and Risk Management:**

   - AI will play a crucial role in ensuring regulatory compliance and managing financial risks. Automated compliance monitoring and advanced risk assessment tools will help wealth managers navigate the complex regulatory environment and protect client assets.

5. **Ethical Considerations and Transparency:**

   • As AI becomes more integrated into wealth management, ethical consider-ations and transparency will be paramount. Ensuring that AI-driven decisions are fair, unbiased, and transparent will be essential for maintaining client trust and confidence.

6. **Education and Training:**

   • The adoption of AI in wealth management will require ongoing education and training for financial professionals. Advisors will need to develop new skills to effectively leverage AI tools and provide value-added services to their clients.

Call to Action

1. **Embrace AI Technology:**

   • Wealth management firms should embrace AI technology to stay competitive and meet the evolving needs of their clients. Investing in AI-driven tools and platforms will enhance operational efficiency and improve client outcomes.

2. **Focus on Client-Centric Solutions:**

   • While leveraging AI, firms must maintain a client-centric approach. Combining AI-driven insights with personalized service will ensure that cli-ents receive tailored and relevant financial advice.

3. **Commit to Continuous Improvement:**

   • The wealth management industry should commit to continuous improvement by staying abreast of technological advancements and evolving client prefer-ences. Regularly updating AI models and training staff will ensure that firms remain at the forefront of innovation.

4. **Promote Ethical AI Practices:**

   • Wealth managers must promote ethical AI practices by ensuring transparency, fairness, and accountability in AI-driven decisions. This will help build and maintain client trust in AI-enhanced financial services.

In conclusion, AI has the potential to revolutionize wealth management by offering unprecedented levels of efficiency, accuracy, and personalization. The integration of AI-driven technologies with traditional wealth management practices will create a more dynamic and client-centric industry. By embracing AI and focusing on continuous improvement, wealth management firms can deliver superior financial solutions and achieve long-term success.

The future of wealth management is bright, with AI playing a pivotal role in shaping the industry. As AI technology continues to evolve, its impact on wealth management will only grow, providing clients with innovative and effective financial strategies. The next chapter will provide a glossary of key terms and concepts in wealth management and AI, offering a valuable resource for readers to deepen their understanding of the topics covered in this book.

Glossary of Key Terms and Concepts[1]

Algorithmic Trading: The use of computer algorithms to execute trades at high speeds and volumes, based on pre-defined criteria and market conditions.

Artificial Intelligence (AI): The simulation of human intelligence in machines that are programmed to think and learn like humans.

Behavioral Finance: The study of psychological factors and biases that influence financial decision-making.

Big Data: Large and complex datasets that require advanced data processing and analysis techniques to extract meaningful insights.

Chatbot: An AI-powered virtual assistant that interacts with users through text or voice, providing real-time information and assistance.

Client Profiling: The process of gathering and analyzing client data to understand their financial situation, preferences, and goals.

Compliance Monitoring: The use of systems and processes to ensure adherence to regulatory requirements and standards.

Data Analytics: The process of analyzing large datasets to uncover patterns, trends, and insights that inform decision-making.

Deep Learning: A subset of machine learning that involves neural networks with many layers, capable of learning from vast amounts of unstructured data.

Descriptive Analytics: The use of historical data to understand past events and performance.

Diagnostic Analytics: The analysis of data to identify the causes of past events and performance.

Environmental, Social, and Governance (ESG) Criteria: A set of standards for evaluating a company's operations and impact on the environment, society, and governance practices.

---

[1] This chapter provides a glossary of key terms and concepts related to wealth management and AI, serving as a valuable resource for readers to deepen their understanding of the topics covered in this book.

© The Editor(s) (if applicable) and The Author(s), under exclusive license to
Springer Nature Switzerland AG 2024
M. Mirghaemi, K. Wendt, *AI Technology in Wealth Management*, SpringerBriefs
in Finance, https://doi.org/10.1007/978-3-031-72223-3

Exchange-Traded Fund (ETF): A type of investment fund that is traded on stock exchanges, holding assets such as stocks, bonds, or commodities.

Financial Goal Setting: The process of defining and prioritizing financial objectives, such as saving for retirement, buying a home, or funding education.

Hybrid Model: A wealth management approach that combines AI-driven tools with the personalized service of human advisors.

Machine Learning: A subset of AI that involves the use of algorithms and statistical models to enable computers to learn from data and improve their performance on specific tasks.

Natural Language Processing (NLP): A branch of AI that enables computers to understand, interpret, and generate human language.

Personalized Financial Advice: Financial recommendations tailored to an individual's unique circumstances, preferences, and goals.

Portfolio Management: The process of managing an investment portfolio to achieve specific financial goals, including asset allocation, rebalancing, and risk management.

Predictive Analytics: The use of statistical models and machine learning algorithms to forecast future events and trends.

Prescriptive Analytics: The use of data-driven insights to recommend specific actions to achieve desired outcomes.

Regulatory Compliance: Adherence to laws, regulations, and standards that govern financial services and transactions.

Risk Assessment: The process of evaluating the risk associated with different investment strategies and financial decisions.

Robo-Advisor: An AI-driven platform that provides automated, algorithm-based portfolio management services with minimal human intervention.

Scenario Analysis: The use of models to simulate various financial scenarios and assess their potential impact on investment portfolios.

Stress Testing: The use of simulations to evaluate how a portfolio or financial system would perform under adverse conditions.

Tax-Loss Harvesting: A strategy to minimize taxes by selling losing investments to offset capital gains from winning investments.

Virtual Assistant: An AI-powered software agent that can perform tasks or services based on user input and context.

References

Brunel, J. L. P. (2015). *Goals-based wealth management: An integrated and practical approach to changing the structure of wealth advisory practices*. Wiley.

Bührer, C. (2005). *Swiss society for financial market research* (pp. 99–108).

Cocca, T. (2016). Potential and limitations of virtual advice in wealth management. *Journal of Financial Transformation*, 45–57.

Das, S. R., et al. (2018). A new approach to goals-based wealth management. *Journal of Investment Management, 16*(3), 1–27.

Devan, M., Tillu, R., & Shanmugam, L. (2023). Federated learning architecture: Design, implementation, and challenges in distributed AI systems. *Journal of Knowledge Learning and Science Technology, 2*(3), 371–384. ISSN: 2959-6386 (Online).

Investopedia. (2024). *Wealth management meaning and what wealth managers charge*.

Kaal, W. A. (2021). Financial technology and hedge funds. In *The Oxford Handbook of Hedge Funds* (pp. 232–250). https://doi.org/10.1093/oxfordhb/9780198840954.013.13

Nuti, G., Mirghaemi, M., Treleaven, P., & Yingsaeree, C. (2011). Algorithmic trading. *Computer, 44*(11), 61–69.

PwC Consulting Research Paper. (2017). *Asset & wealth management revolution: Embracing exponential change*.

Singh, I., & Kaur, N. (2017). Wealth management through robo advisory. *International Journal of Research -Granthaalayah, 5*(6), 33–43. https://doi.org/10.29121/granthaalayah. v5.i6.2017.1991

The Investors Book. (2024). *What is wealth management? Definition, process, strategies, benefits, tips*.

Ting, H.-I. (2017). Factors affecting wealth management services: From investors' and advisors' perspectives. *The Journal of Wealth Management, 20*(1), 17–29.

References